How the Critics Can Help

ERIC FRANKLIN

How the Critics Can Help

*A Guide to the Practical Use of
the Gospels*

SCM PRESS LTD

BS
2530
. F72
1982

334 02058 1

First published 1982
by SCM Press Ltd
58 Bloomsbury Street, London

Typeset by Gloucester Typesetting Services
and printed in Great Britain by
Richard Clay Ltd (The Chaucer Press)
Bungay, Suffolk

To the memory of
Geoffrey Lampe, gospel critic
and
John Fielder, parish priest
Two ministers of the New Covenant

CONTENTS

PROLOGUE

The Preacher and the Critic

For the past five years or so I have been exercising something of a dual ministry as a curate on the staff of an urban parish and as a part-time teacher of the New Testament in both an established theological college and a newly founded school of ministry. This dual role has pinpointed the problem of the relation between the academic and the practical, between the work of the gospel critic, whose ideas and researches it has been my concern to try to unravel and to interpret, and that of the parish priest whose pastoral obligations it has been my privilege to try to understand and to share. And there does seem to be a very real tension between the two. How can the parish priest use the insights of the scholar, aware as he is of the responsibility he has to the congregation he is privileged to serve and of the needs as well as the love of those who become very much a part of his life and of his very being? Does the work of the critic have anything to say to him that can effectively enable the gospel to run more freely among them? More especially, should what the scholars are saying influence and inform his preaching and, if it should, how can it?

It must be admitted at once that the value and relevance of the work of the biblical critic for the general practitioner is not obviously self-evident. Many a generation of ordinands has left the academic study of the gospels behind them with an all too audible sigh of relief. The hours spent on source criticism, on form criticism, and more recently on redaction criticism have not made an obvious mark on the way they handle the gospels when they prepare their sermons. The academic is seen as apart from the practical, the work of the student as having little to offer once student days are over and those of the pastor have begun. I can remember a theological college principal in one sermon class expostulating fiercely with one student, who was an honours graduate in theology, and demanding to know how his study of the New Testament had been drawn into the service of the sermon. Certainly there was no indication of its use. And I can remember the student's exasperation at the onslaught, the justice of which was not immediately granted simply because the relevance of those studies was not immediately obvious. The penny had not dropped, not because the student was either dim or disinterested, but because it simply was not self-evident that there was a penny there to drop. It is not always the student's fault, and the burden of proof, the responsibility for carrying conviction, lies firmly with the biblical critics themselves. The ordinand, and indeed the ordained man, must not be left unable to see the wood for the multitude of the trees, and minute details must be seen to contribute to the broad sweep which is needed to widen his vision and stir his imagination.[1]

However, even if the importance of the biblical critic's work be granted – even if the critic's own understanding of its significance be accepted and its relevance be appreciated – the practical applications may still be doubted or denied. Can his conclusions really be used by the preacher? Indeed, more than that, are they compatible with Christianity as he and his congregation (and, we might add, his church) understand it? Many critics maintain that their work inevitably alters the faith of those who accept their conclusions, but do they actually undermine it and, in fact, destroy it? The penny of relevance may have dropped but, on closer inspection, does it turn out to be either a devalued coin or even a totally alien currency? On the face of it, at any rate, the outlook of the biblical critic presents very real difficulties to the preacher as he faces his pastoral responsibilities.

In the first place, the results of modern criticism, as they permeate out to the preacher, seem to be largely negative and to have little to offer him as he strives to present something positive to his congregation to help them face the difficult business of Christian believing and living in the modern world. Central to this is, what at any rate appears on the face of it to be, the modern critic's attack on the historical reliability of the gospels. The preacher is told that the gospels are not biographies and that it is not possible to write a life of Jesus. He hears the term 'myth' used in connection with them and is informed that they represent Jesus, not as he really was, but as he was seen to be through the preaching of the early church in the light of the rise of its resurrection faith. The preacher has long lived uncomfortably with the miracles but now he is told that the gospels do not necessarily bear witness to the historicity of the virgin birth and that the Easter narratives do not necessarily mean that Jesus' bones may not still be lying, undisturbed by God or man, in some unknown Palestinian grave.

All this inevitably calls into question the more general understanding of the significance of the gospel accounts and therefore of their authority. An attitude which casts doubts upon the historical veracity of the biblical contents must put a question mark against the importance and authority of the biblical beliefs expressed through them. Belief in revelation seems to take a hard knock. The parish priest's background, the theological assumptions of his church and its credal and near-credal statements, his congregation's beliefs, and the expressions of faith permeating the worship in which the sermon is set – all these combine to give the Bible an authority which comes close to that given to it by the movement labelled as Biblical Theology which itself has probably contributed much to the preacher's own theological position and which determines the mode and direction of his pastoral ministry.

Biblical Theology stressed the unity of the biblical outlook which permeated its various parts and therefore enabled the whole to be given an authority which impressed by its massive coherence and commanded adherence by its impressiveness. The distinctiveness of the biblical outlook was seized upon as isolating it from the vicissitudes and chances of its cultural setting. Hebrew thought was contrasted with Greek to bring out its superiority and to allow it to be seen as an altogether adequate medium through which the revelation of God could be communicated to men. The biblical outlook was therefore declared as normative for the expression of the Christian faith which was seen to rest on assured facts (even if they were hazy in their details) as they were interpreted by an impressive consistency. The preacher's word therefore had behind it a formidable support and he could work within a framework of thought which produced a large number of very fine studies of biblical themes – of the biblical doctrines of creation, of man, of work, of the work of Christ, and so on.

The work of the biblical critic has shattered this confidence in the Bible's uniquely privileged position. Biblical Theology is now declared to have been over-confident in its historical conclusions, and to have arrived at its estimate of the unity of the Bible by somewhat artificial means which ignored rough edges by playing down the individuality of its many parts. It is under attack for having underestimated the cultural, social, and religious influences bearing upon the various authors. Its search for distinctiveness is regarded as something of an alien intrusion upon the real webs of biblical thought, and its belief in the normative value of the scriptures is therefore called severely into question. The necessity to embrace Hebrew thought in a scientific age may have brought difficulties, but at least it gave coherence, a scheme, a clear-cut framework for the expression of Christianity. Its very distinctiveness in the twentieth century seemed to enhance its god-givenness and to allow a clear definition of Christian belief. But now the clarity and the unity are gone, and with them, not only a certain distinctive otherworldliness, but also the authority and confidence which they enabled.[2]

In all this the work of the biblical critic seems to be negative and so constitutes a very real difficulty for the preacher. It is perhaps the fundamental difficulty for him, but if he still perseveres in his attempt to see what of a positive nature it has to offer, he soon faces a further problem, namely that occasioned by the very diversity of the biblical critics' conclusions. He will meet very different evaluations of the significance of the biblical material, of its historical value, of the meaning of its statements and of the aims of its authors. Getting behind the biblical, and especially the gospel, records remains a hazardous enterprise and a search for a way in to the various narratives seems often to be leading to a whole succession of blind alleys. On any question he will be faced with a bewildering multiplicity of views. Certainties are nil, probabilities few, but possibilities endless. The confidence with which a biblical critic disseminates his own conclusions is inevitably negatived by the equal confidence with which some other critic propounds a diametrically opposed point of view. It is therefore hardly surprising if the preacher expresses little confidence in either! He will remember that God is a God, not of confusion but of peace, and he will wonder if the Holy Spirit's activity is really to be discerned in such diversity.

And yet again he will remember that the biblical critics are only human and are all too often influenced by the dictates of the age in which they live. He will be aware that theological fashions change with a disturbing frequency and that what is propounded as the answer for one generation is quickly denied, and all too frequently denounced by the next. The liberal Jesus, the apocalyptic fanatic, the biblically theological Christ, the social redeemer, the mythological saviour, the revolutionary leader – to name but a few – have all come and gone and none has brought that finality, that divine vindication, which it promised. What rock can the preacher find on which to build among the sands of seemingly endless speculation and reconstruction? What faith can he have that the latest position will prove itself to be more permanent than its predecessors? Is the present position just unduly sceptical, drawing on the scepticism of the age, consciously or unconsciously reflecting that failure of nerve which he sees around him in so many of the church's enterprises? What does such writing allow him to say to strengthen and encourage the faith of his congregation? That it has anything at all to say is not obvious.

The parish priest may well feel that the pastoral implications of much of their writing have not been really thought through by a large number of modern scholars and he may well believe that his own instinct for what is in keeping with the gospel as he sees it actually at work among men may make many of their conclusions suspect or in fact rule them out of court. He may wish the theoretical framework of the scholarly discussion to be tested, and indeed tempered by, the realities of the church and the world as he sees these open to the moving Spirit of God in their midst.

Nevertheless, the preacher will not lightly turn aside from the critics' work. He cannot deny that it is happening, that many will hear of its results, and that not a few will be helped by its conclusions. Its discussions have been taken out of the confines of the lecture room, have been aired on television with a response which shows that they ring bells with many people, and have begun to enter into the more popular literature of the paperbacks. The simple fact is that television on a Sunday evening is no longer the preserve of the traditionalist, and paperback religious guidance is not solely in the hands (capable though they are) of William Barclay. Moreover, religious education is not completely defunct in schools but will if it is to survive use more and more of the phenomenological approach. It will be descriptive of man's attempts to find satisfaction and fulfilment in this business of living, and will by this method seek to achieve its hopes of giving the youngsters a 'faith to live by' or a 'stance for living'. It will not ignore the results of the biblical critics' work as it seeks to present Christianity as believed and practised by its followers but will inevitably show its students the different ways in which the Christian faith is understood and expressed. And this discussion of Christianity is not confined to the young. When I recently talked to a group of Toc H women, I did the kind of thing I would normally avoid doing, because of its negative attitude, and stated that I did not, I thought, believe in angels. So far from the response being hostile, as I expected, it was rather one of relief. It freed the discussion so that it could concentrate upon the real challenge of Christianity, and it enabled the real and necessary stumbling-block to be seen uncluttered by unnecessary obstacles.

Many of these people are to be found in the pews as well as in discussion groups and they are easily offended by an ignoring or an all too easy rejection of what seems true, or at least very possible, to them. The preacher can no longer afford to ignore the critic's work or to reject it too easily if he is to carry conviction. Even if he is to disagree with it – even to the extent of attacking its fundamental presuppositions – he can only do so effectively if he has entered into real dialogue with it and has tried to understand its outlook sympathetically.

And the preacher will be aware of the need of new ways to make the Bible real to his congregation. We may give honour to it with our gospel processions, we may all respond with gratitude to the proclamation that 'This is the word of the Lord', but in reality, except in those places where there is a community which has been gripped by the Bible conservatively explained or for those individuals who have really used it with various aids, its actual impact upon our congregations is minimal. It is not really a live option for them. Its message does not impinge upon them with any real relevance. It does not make an effective witness to them. The Bible has to be rescued from indifference shrouded in that respect normally reserved for ancient monuments.[3]

Two illustrations of this seem to stand out clearly. Every year at Advent we continue to use the Bible's proclamation of an imminent End and of the nearness of the coming of the Son of Man. We read the gospel statements, we continue these in our prayers, and we elaborate them in our hymns. But we cannot hope to share in the actual biblical faith by doing this for none of us seriously contemplates the imminent return of Christ so that we live controlled by the expectation in some way resembling the control it exercised over Paul when he wrote, say, I Corinthians. Two thousand years of continuing history cannot be so easily ignored. But the result is that we cling to the imagery at the expense of learning anything real from the biblical expectation. Our belief cannot be the same as that of biblical times, but it should at least be seeking to learn from their expectations, really to see what they meant for them, and to see how, in different times and circumstances and with beliefs that are different from theirs, they might still contribute something vital to our Christian faith. As it is we pay lip service to a kind of fundamentalism and ignore totally a kerygma.

The Christmas story presents problems which are not altogether different. Any parish priest must come away from the Midnight Mass both uplifted and downcast. He is uplifted by the commemoration of the birth of Christ and by the appeal this has to produce such large congregations. But he is downcast by the thought, not only that many of them will not be in church again until next year, but more so by the certainty that the full impact of the Christmas proclamation will not have impinged upon the vast majority of those present. The impact upon most of them will have been through the Christmas story. But the original proclamation through the story is now changed into one of harmony, peacefulness, and tranquility. It is sentimentalized into an expression of people's longings, into an expression of something evoking the best in man rather than proclaiming the reality of God's approach to men.

The fact is that the Bible, when given a surface interpretation, does not challenge as it ought. It has no real chance of entering into the faith-experience of a large part of our congregations so that it neither enriches, deepens, stirs, or moves. It has become tamed, domesticated, instantly dissolved without lumps – and lost. Even the teaching of Jesus is not easily presented. How often are we clergy begged to stick to the 'simple teaching' of the Sermon on the Mount and assured of its relevance and inbuilt power to commend itself? But how, for instance, does one when faced with the scepticism of public schoolboys at their compulsory Sunday service, preach on the passage 'Take no thought for the morrow . . .' in the light of the realities of modern life so that it comes even faintly near to the significance it had for Jesus and the early church? How can it in any way be a real vehicle for the gospel unless this can in fact be done? The past is no longer regarded as virtuous for its own sake; it no longer has an authority of its own unless it can meet and enter into real dialogue with the present. It becomes real, it becomes authoritative, only as it is seen to have had a validity for its contemporaries, and as it meets the present, not by overwhelming it, but by engaging it, and so by helping to free it for the future.

Modern criticism of the Bible helps towards this end. It seeks to open up the biblical witness in order to allow it to meet the present. It seeks to allow the Bible to speak for itself, in its own terms, and under its own canons, and it allows that the right answers can only have the remotest chance of being heard if the right questions are asked of it in the first place.

At this point one further problem has to be faced. The biblical critics may all be asking the same questions, but they certainly do not all come up with the same answers. There are critics and critics, and it is not this time just a question of how different parts of the evidence are evaluated, it is rather a different 'feel', a different hunch, a different way of looking at the whole. It is affected by one's background, teachers, experience, and even to some extent by one's personality as well as by one's scholarly judgments. Together, these influence the way any critic looks at the gospels, the expectations that he brings to them, the way he is moved by them. Every critic has to come to terms with the New Testament so as to be able to find integrity both in it and in himself. But, as he does this, he is drawn into a particular position in relation to modern critical views which, though it has to be his own and draws from the insights and results of various outlooks, inevitably feels more 'in tune' with scholars of one particular approach than with those who represent other points of view.

Preaching however is a sharing of convictions, a commending of those things by which one feels grasped. The manner in which the immediate subject is proclaimed is determined inevitably by one's apprehension of the whole gospel. In the same way, how one faces and resolves particular problems raised by gospel criticism – for example the historicity of individual narratives – is usually determined, not by issues affecting that incident alone, but by attitudes derived from one's overall 'feel' which has itself been formed by one's total study. It is the overall outlook which these pages seek to commend.

For that outlook does, I believe, arise out of true insights into the meaning and significance of the four gospels. And it has not really been given a fair hearing by most of us in the parishes. For I remain convinced not only of the fact that those critics, whose work when viewed from a distance might seem disturbing, have discovered true insights into the significance of the gospels, but also that they have something of great value to offer the preacher as he exercises his role of pastor and missionary. The work of the critics can enable the Bible to be rediscovered and to become a vital force in the presentation of the gospel. It can enable a rediscovery of truly biblical preaching.

For many a preacher has come to feel uncomfortable with the gospels. They represent a tool which he finds himself unable to use with confidence simply because he is no longer sure of the purpose for which it is designed. They represent an outlook which is other than his own, speaking of a world which is hardly his world, with expectations far removed from his. It is not enough to say that human nature is unchanged, for human nature itself is compounded of outlooks, instincts, expectations, convictions, temptations, beliefs, and experiences none of which meets us in the same way as it met the evangelists and their readers. The world, people, life itself, and even the God behind life, have taken on a different complexion. Many a preacher instinctively feels that one cannot pass straight from the gospels to the modern world without introducing unreality either into the gospels or into the world in which he lives. Our experience is not theirs: therefore our expectations and theirs just do not coincide. Many an ordained man, not long out of college, has admitted to me how he has been unable as a preacher to relate to the gospels. He has had, if not a failure of nerve, then at least a failure of conviction, of commitment to them. Faced with an episode in the life of Jesus, be it a biographical narrative, a miracle story, a piece of teaching, sometimes even a parable, he has not been able to engage it so that it can become in his hands a proclamation of the saving grace of God. Whereas his understanding of life as well as his intellectual quest had led him towards the position taken up by the biblical critic, that very critic's work has not offered a way into the gospels to release them as a channel of the gospel itself. So there has come about a death of real biblical preaching and there has been no real link between the gospel passage and the sermon which is projected on to it.

This, I hasten to add, is in no way a criticism of the preacher. It is rather a statement of the problem which the work of the modern critic has made even more acute. For the critic should not be surprised if the preacher, when challenged by his conclusions, should look upon them as at best a blessing which is very well disguised! To the preacher who is also a pastor, the work of the gospel critic presents him in fact with what may most realistically be described as something of a mixed blessing. It really is a case of something like the curate's egg. That his use of the critic's work will enable the gospel to run free is undoubtedly true, but it will do so not without making heavy demands upon him and his thinking and will not leave him without some heartache as he strives to use his insights with hope and sensitivity and as he tries to put these before his congregation and so to deepen their faith which so often surpasses, judges, and rebukes his own.

These chapters, then, are addressed in the first place to those who are slightly (or more than slightly) uncomfortable, to those who have an element of dissatisfaction in themselves about their use of the gospels. They are concerned with those who instinctively feel that there might be something real in what the critics are saying, who sense that there is something of a gap between the Bible as it is often traditionally understood and life as it is experienced today.[4] Yet they remain equally uncomfortable with the critics' work for, though it strikes chords with them, it leaves them unsure of its usefulness, even of its correctness, in their pastoral concerns. So they avoid it in the pulpit and feel uncertain and unco-ordinated as a result.

But it is my hope too that these chapters will have something to say to those who have been somewhat dismissive of the critics' work. This is more difficult for it at once leaves their author open to the charge of pride – of seeming either patronizing or superior – as well as to that of insensitivity. But the risk must be taken, not only because I believe that this approach has something to contribute to that seeking after truth on which we are all engaged, but also because the critic himself needs the criticisms of those who look at his work through eyes formed by pastoral concerns. A real dialogue between the critic and the man in the field is long overdue.

Our first task then will be to try to uncover and to summarize what the biblical critics are saying about the gospels – about their nature, purpose, the things that contributed to their production and to the people who produced them – and to see how this must affect our use of them as preaching tools and yardsticks for our understanding of Jesus. However, because such an understanding arouses in an acute form the question of the relation of the gospels to history, chapter four must be concerned with this. It is in fact *the* problem since it raises questions about the nature of Christian claims which can be most distressing to the Christian community. A consideration of these questions brings us then to the problem caused by the fact that the outlook of the evangelists is very different from our own. Chapter five, therefore, has to be concerned with the question of how the message of the gospels can actually inform and deepen our message, of how the words of the evangelists can become a word of God for us and, through us, to our congregations. We then consider specific problems presented to us when we try to preach Jesus of Nazareth – how the Jesus who walked in Galilee is less accessible to us than we would like and perhaps less immediately appealing than many modern and partial presentations of him would suggest. After this, we look at the infancy narratives, the resurrection narratives, and the miracle stories to try to discover how these can be used by us today. Finally, we bring our work to a conclusion by trying to suggest how all this should affect our proclamation of the gospel and what it adds to a fuller understanding of the significance of Jesus. We suggest that the pain and the travail inherent in assimilating the valid insights in what the critics are saying to us can actually produce a deeper response to the God who calls us, and that they therefore have a claim to be heard by the church at large.

I

The Critics and the Gospels I: Behind the Gospels

The outstandingly positive contribution of modern criticism towards a better understanding of the gospels has been to set them firmly within the life and beliefs of the early church. That they must be seen in relation to the whole life of the church is of course no new emphasis. Generations of teachers have explained how the community existed before the gospels came into being and how the life and witness of the church are to be seen as both illuminating and confirming the faith which is proclaimed through the written word.

Nevertheless, the full implications of this insight were not really followed through. The church by and large was seen as the interpreter of the Bible which was in fact allowed to stand apart from her and which was in practice viewed almost as a separate entity existing in its own God-given right. So the authors of the gospels were not really treated as part and parcel of the church, building upon her witness and related to her by both their background, their message, and their concerns. They were in fact treated as though they were isolated from the community and were regarded as doing their writing either upon a cloud suspended half-way between heaven and earth or within a study conducive to determined and objective research, but insulated from the hopes and problems of those outside. The result was that the gospels came to be regarded either as untouched by human hands or as unrelated to life in the raw. They had not been assimilated into a faith whose yardstick of truth is belief in an incarnation and which therefore should be suspicious of any saving action which is not rooted in real human thinking and living.

The work of the modern critic has enabled us to counter the deficiencies of this kind of thinking. The gospels are now seen as part and parcel of the young church, drawing upon its life, created by its being, expressing its faith, and addressing its fears. Behind them lie some thirty years of life in the founding Christian community which was brought into being by the ministry, death, and resurrection of Jesus of Nazareth, a community which was forced to work out his significance for them and the nature of their response to him in a world which was nearly always problematical and often downright hostile. Behind the gospels, shaping their individual parts and determining the nature of the whole, there lies a community whose beliefs, aspirations, fears and failings have gone into the making of living testimonies. The gospels are witnesses to the fact that men have been grasped by God in Christ; they are in fact proclamations of their responses to him in ever new and changing situations.[1]

The attention of the critics in this connection was directed in the first instance, not to the gospels as wholes, but to the individual incidents, to the separate stories which seem to have been strung together, often loosely connected to their contexts and occupying different places in the various gospels. It was the individual units which came under the spotlight of those scholars who came to be known as form critics. Form criticism viewed the written narratives as the end product of a number of years of oral tradition. The form critics therefore attempted to go behind the written narratives, to recreate the situations in which the stories had been passed on by word of mouth, and to assess how their settings in the church's life had actually shaped and influenced the ways in which the different kinds of stories were told.

Overall, the form critics have had a bad press in England. They undoubtedly exaggerated the creative role of the church and were over-confident in their assertions of its main concerns. They tended to overlook the fact that eyewitnesses of the life of Jesus themselves contributed to the church's understanding of him and that these were unlikely to have forgotten the significance of what had happened in his ministry. They therefore underplayed the church's concern with what had happened then and its necessary interest in 'How it all began' and 'How we got where we are'.[2]

Nevertheless they were completely justified in their assertion that the resurrection brought about a new awareness on the part of Jesus' disciples and that this inevitably influenced the way in which the events of his life were 'seen' and told. Jesus was now experienced as a living, contemporary presence and stories of his past life were therefore told in such a way that they inevitably reflected the beliefs, hopes and fears of the present. We allow the beliefs of the present to influence our telling of the past. The intensity of the early church's experience and the sense of newness that this brought made it all the more inevitable with them.

Their concern with the present and their belief in Jesus as their living, vital, contemporary Lord affected the early Christians' story-telling in three ways. Firstly, it meant that they were selective. As the final comment of the Fourth Gospel maintains, 'There are also many other things which Jesus did; were every one of them to be written, I suppose that the world itself could not contain the books that would be written.' Those that are recorded were retained precisely because of their significance for the later church: 'Now Jesus did many other signs in the presence of the disciples, which are not written in this book: but these are written that you may believe that Jesus is the Christ, the Son of God, and that believing you may have life in his name.' The early church appears to have had very little interest in biographical details for their own sake for, if it had, it would undoubtedly have sought out the stories of Jesus' childhood, of his developing understanding of his inner life. But it did neither of these things and we consequently lack essential information which would be needed to fulfil anything like the requirements of modern biographical concern.

Secondly, their use by the early church shaped many of the stories so that biographical details were often subordinated to, or sometimes even excluded by, the point which was wanted to be made through the telling of the story. The story was used as much to serve the church's concerns – its beliefs, conflicts, fears, hopes, and liturgical interests – as it was to relate an incident in Jesus' life. The past was used, inevitably, in the service of the present, and the needs of the present often controlled the manner in which the past was told.

In the third place, form criticism says that because the stories were used in the service of the church, the response of the early church to Jesus was often read back into them. Events in the life of Jesus were often filled with an Easter dimension so that the post-resurrection out-look of the early church was carried back into the pre-resurrection situation. Events in the life of Jesus were given a significance which was not necessarily obvious to those who had been with him and they were filled with a content which was enriched by the experiences and faith of those who lived in his power. The faith of those who told the stories made this inevitable as they saw for the first time the reality of what had happened in his life.

Selectivity, emphasis, and creativity – these were present in the early church's telling of stories of Jesus and these enabled her to make them into vital and direct proclamations about him as he grasped them in the present. Nevertheless, it is important to remember that what she did is not so very different from what we do today. We are of course limited in our freedom, and our creative capacities are controlled by the fact that we have the stories in a written and therefore in a static form. But within these limitations we tend to let the present exercise a fair amount of control over the past. In spite of its murdering of the text, we still let our wise men go to the stable. This does away not only with the awkward task of converting our Christmas stable into a house but it becomes a vehicle for our natural desire to make Matthew's and Luke's infancy narratives into an harmonious unity. For teachers it provides a unified approach to the whole symbolism of the nativity. Again, and quite without biblical authority, we add the presence of animals to our crib scene. Our teaching concerns make us call the honoured visitors kings rather than wise men, for whereas kings can sum-up and represent the whole activity of the Gentile world, wise men somehow get lost beneath possibilities of their being statesmen or astrologers or intellectuals or charlatans or bits of all rolled into one. Teaching possibilities, belief, and perhaps even convenience and the desire for a good, meaningful story (dare we say even sentimentality?) have been allowed to cloud the expression of hard facts.

And aren't we selective? How often do we make use of the awkward bits of the gospels? When we do, don't we in fact try to smooth down the rough edges? How many of us, unbidden, choose to preach on the parable of the rogue steward or on the story of the healing of the Syrophoenician woman's daughter? If we recount the latter, don't we inevitably gloss over its harsh reality by bringing in a (hoped for) sense of humour on the part of Jesus, or else go on to talk about little dogs, household dogs, as though that gave dignity to the poor woman who knelt before him?

And don't our liturgical concerns – our present beliefs and our congregational needs – influence us in our understanding of the past and what it contained? Many of us week by week recount the Anglican Communion Series 3 version of the events at the Last Supper as they are included in the great Thanksgiving Prayer, yet we are not conscious that it is in fact a composite account which does not actually reflect any one New Testament version of the event. The words we use are an up-dating of what is found in the Book of Common Prayer which, departing from the very free recital contained in the Latin canon, was based upon St Paul's description contained in I Corinthians 11. Yet it is not a

complete following of that account. From Mark it includes Jesus'
command to take bread and it then, quite without biblical authority,
repeats this for the cup. From Matthew it adds 'for the forgiveness of
sins' to the explanation of the cup's significance. These are additions
which the Pauline version lacks and can be justified on the grounds that
Paul was, quite simply, unaware of them. No such simple explanation,
however, is possible for justifying the departure from the Pauline version of the meaning of the cup and its replacement by the Markan
report. Paul has 'This cup is the new covenant in my blood'. Presumably such a version might have been hard for some of Cranmer's
congregations to accept, and the Prayer Book goes to the more familiar
Markan account, 'This is my blood of the (new) covenant which is
poured out for many', but which it elaborates by drawing upon both
Paul and Matthew.

What the Eucharistic Prayer retells is determined primarily, not by
the quest for historical accuracy, but by what is most meaningful for
the present. Liturgical relevance and the need to draw out the significance of the event for the later worshippers have determined how the
institution is actually narrated and it seems that these considerations
have left their mark on the actual New Testament descriptions. Paul's
account represents what has been called 'a precipitate of Jesus' words
percolated through the mind of a rabbi' whilst Mark's represents one
which is controlled by the church's looking for the early coming of the
kingdom of God, an account which Matthew has slightly altered in the
interests of his more established congregation. Luke's episode is complicated by strong textual variations but at least one of them (the
'shorter text') represents a tradition which is very distinctive in that the
cup precedes the bread and is wholly eschatological in its interests.
There is no mention of any incorporation into benefits derived from
Christ's death.

What the early witnesses include – how they actually recount the
episode – seems to be determined less by their interest in what actually
happened than by their concern that it should be relevant to their contemporaries. It is perhaps unlikely that the evangelists themselves
altered the tradition they received, because to have done so at such a
sensitive and immediately familiar point in the narrative would have
been to invite the disapproval of their fellow-churchmen. They were
reflecting the liturgical use of their own particular church and it is this
which has shaped the narrative to make it what it is now. But that it has
been shaped is undeniable. Paul himself points to his own place in the

tradition of the church. He proclaims that he is handing on what has actually been handed down to him and that such a procedure guarantees that what is given really is derived from the Lord – 'For I received from the Lord what I also delivered to you' (I Cor. 11.23). This represents a tradition which claims to go back to Jesus, but it must also have been one which allows the risen Christ to speak in and through the tradition as it is shaped and developed by its place in the ongoing life of the church. The Lord speaks not only in the original words of Jesus but also in the living creative tradition behind those words as they are handed down. The Lord is not just a figure of the past but a creative presence in the corporate experience of the Christian community. This means that when Paul talks of a 'word of the Lord' it is not always clear whether he refers to a saying of Jesus or to one given, perhaps through a prophet, in the continuing life of the church. The attitude was not a free and easy one, and sayings were not made up willy-nilly to suit the convenience and wishes of the church, but that there was this creative situation which both adds to, and so inevitably clouds, the words of Jesus in his actual time on earth is incontestable.

But, again, this represents an attitude which is not totally other than our own. For the fact is that we do not come to the New Testament gospels without our presuppositions and these inevitably colour and even determine what we actually hear when we listen to these remarkable documents. We read the gospels through eyes which are influenced by our part in the church of the twentieth century, by the beliefs of that church, by its worship, by our own experience of the living Christ, and by the need we have to relate all that to our lives as Christians, and we quite unconsciously transform what is there in the text before us so that it fits into our total picture of the living Lord who meets as where we are. This is quite inevitable and is a process which is similar to that which actually influenced the evangelists as they wrote and was indeed influencing the telling and receiving of the stories before ever they came to be written down.

And we do it quite unconsciously and totally unaware that we are acting in a manner which might in any way be judged illegitimate. For our knowledge in the present ultimately controls what we 'see' in the past. It is even allowed to determine what we declare to have happened in the past for it is ultimately our present faith which is allowed a very large share in determining what was appropriate for then. We know the Lord who is and the past is therefore no closed book to us. Past and present merge into one and experience becomes the criterion of the truths of both.

What then is the significance of all this for our use of the gospels? How does it mean that we are to approach the stories of Jesus? What have they to say to us? Our usual approach to the gospels is to see them as information about the life of Jesus. We try to reconstruct what happened then, to see what such a story about the past can say to us as we try to make it come alive and then to apply what we learn about this to our daily lives. We try to look at him as though we were contemporary with his earthly life. Now this of itself is not necessarily a wrong approach (even though we must be aware of its limitations when we use it). 'Jesus as he really was' cannot be divorced from our present concerns. But the work of the modern gospel critic reminds us that, if this is our concern, then we must proceed with caution for, since it does not seem to have been the main concern of the early Christian generations, they have left us with material which cannot immediately and easily satisfy us. What we have in the gospels is Jesus as seen through the eyes of the early church and as illuminated by the light of their own understanding of him. What he was for them has to be our source for working out both what in fact he was and also what he can become for us. The first practical result of the form critics' work is to remind us of the nature of the witness that we have before us and to warn us to handle it with care.

But it reminds us also that when we look upon the gospels as responses to the whole work of the living Lord, we are in fact putting the emphasis where the early church placed it and that we are therefore likely to be putting it in the right place. For it is the risen Jesus, not the one who walked in Palestine, who saves, and our acceptance of the narratives as responses to the whole Jesus will enable them to become more direct and immediate channels of his present activity in us. For every event in the life of Jesus must be looked at in the light of the cross and resurrection. Mark's gospel is well aware of this for its author is constantly pointing out the inability of both the disciples and the crowds to understand Jesus. John makes this even more explicit. The true significance of the events in the life of Jesus becomes clear only after his exaltation. 'When therefore he was raised from the dead, his disciples remembered that he had said this, and they believed the scriptures and the word which Jesus had spoken.' So the Johannine Christ promises the Spirit who 'will take what is mine and declare it to you'. The gospels know nothing of that modern yearning to go back to see Jesus as he was in Palestine and to find grace, salvation, and truth in a response to him as he was then. They know only too well that he was an enigma to his contemporaries and that it is only in the light of their corporate experience of his risen presence in the early church that he is really known and understood.

For it is as Lord of our lives, as the one through whom we have been grasped by the whole presence of God, that he must be preached. The Bible itself knows nothing of that older liberal gospel of Jesus as the preacher of the Fatherhood of God and of the infinite value of the human soul. In the hands of a master this kind of understanding was eloquent and attractive.[3] But it could not last simply because it could not satisfy as an adequate interpretation of what the early church knew had happened in its midst. Those young Christians knew that in Jesus God had acted to give them life, release, faith and a future. They had not grasped either God or an ideal; they themselves had been grasped by God, and their accounts of Jesus were impregnated by this fact. Yet much of our use of the gospels still meets many of our contemporaries in the old liberal light. Jesus is set out as an example to be followed or as one who can move us as he moved his companions during his lifetime. Jesus is proclaimed through the incidents of the gospels as less than the resurrected one in our midst and the response which is demanded is less than that of one who is grasped by his risen life, of one who is invited to share in the faith of that young community which, brought into being by what had happened in its midst, grew so that it now incorporates us as it challenges us with its faith and life. And the reason for this is often our desire to stand alongside him in Galilee to embrace him as an easily identified, easily assimilated figure. But he then ceases to be the living Lord. It is forgotten that faith in him was beaten out on the anvil of the cross and resurrection, and was found in the community of those whose hearts had been grasped – that means wrenched, shaken, transformed as they were remade – by God himself. What we therefore proclaim must be, not a message, but an encounter.

We use the gospels to be able to share in the life and experience of the young community as she exalted in his presence and as she faced the problems which such an experience brought. We seek to link our faith and our experience to theirs and so to have our own enriched and deepened. We never forget that both we and they stand this side of the resurrection. We learn first from their faith, from their experience of having been seized by him, from their convictions as they proclaimed him through their stories about him, from their striving to come to terms with and to understand the full nature of what had taken hold of them. We learn from their certainty that they had been taken hold of by God himself and so had been incorporated into his full, complete, active, powerful redemption. God had encountered them in the whole event of Jesus. It is the reality of that encounter to which the gospels witness and which they encourage us to share. They encourage us to stand along-side them, to 'see' as they 'see', to live in the response that they are making.

But we are to learn too not merely from the faith of the early church but also from its fears. If this form of their witness is to be seen in the gospels primarily when they are taken as wholes, it is nevertheless not absent from the early church's handling of the individual stories.

The stories of Jesus' conflicts are told in such a way as to cause light to bear upon the problems of the early church. The young community's relationships with the Jews, its difficulties with the Roman powers, its internal tensions brought about by differing approaches to the law of Moses and the measure of the freedom from that law brought about by Christ – all these and many other concerns are encompassed by the early church's telling of stories about Jesus. Above all, it reflected the early Christian concern with working out the true significance of Jesus – of trying to unpack the full implications of their experience of new life through him. Encounters of Jesus with those who opposed him, dis-closures to those who were struggling to follow him, and healings of those who were shut off from God's creative and saving activity – all these were told to illuminate and undergird the Christian proclamation of what was being experienced through his risen life.

These stories point to the early church in dialogue with the fact of Jesus. They show them facing their difficulties in the light of faith. Basically, their problems were of two kinds, both of which rose out of the particular nature of God's action in Jesus of Nazareth. In the first place, there was the problem of the cross and therefore of the life which led up to it. Jesus was rejected by the Jews, not only during his lifetime but, far more seriously, after his resurrection also. And it was this second Jewish rejection which brought the problem of the cross to the fore. The scandal of the cross was countered by an appeal to the scrip-tures which could be gleaned for texts which seemingly validated a belief in a crucified Messiah. In the hands of the early church, the Old Testament became a book which pointed to Jesus and spoke about him on every page. But the Jews – the people of the book – rejected such an interpretation and this, inevitably, undermined Christian confidence. An answer could only be found by stressing Jewish perversity and blindness. We can see Paul wrestling with this problem in Romans 9–11

and the author of Acts makes it one of his chief concerns. It was a continuing difficulty and the perversity of the Jews became an early Christian theme which has shaped the gospels' stories of Jesus' dealings with
those who were devoted to the law. A stridency in these stories has often
been pointed out and it is no doubt caused, not only by the situation
which met Jesus himself during his ministry, but more so by that which
confronted Christians in the succeeding generations. The 'Jewish problem' faces us in almost every narrative in the gospels. Its ramifications
spread out into almost every aspect of the young church's life.[4]

The second problem arose also out of the cross and of the indirect
vindication provided by the resurrection. Jesus was a hidden Lord. Life
went on, persecutions started, rejections continued. Life for the early
Christians was threatening and they longed for a clear open justification
of their beliefs; they sighed for the Lord to be revealed. 'Come, Lord
Jesus' was the constant cry of the vast majority who went to make up the
early Christian community. And such was the reality of their hope that
they expected its early vindication in an event for all to see. They looked
for the early return of the Lord, for his 'coming on the clouds with
power and great glory'. Since they saw his resurrection as the beginning
of the general resurrection expected at the end, they awaited the
parousia as an imminent event. So, many of Paul's letters have to deal
with the delay and the resulting problems but he nevertheless does so
in a way which shows that he still expects it to occur in his lifetime.

The early church awaited the parousia with hope and, when it did not
happen, when faith in Jesus was not openly vindicated, her members
had to rethink their earlier certainties, to try to come to a better understanding of Jesus' true significance, and to work out more fully the real
implications of the life, death and resurrection of their Lord. In the
gospels, we are privileged to watch them doing this.[5]

We gain by coming to the gospel records through the life of the early
church for we are closer to them in outlook than we are to the situation
that prevailed during the earthly life of Jesus. Like them we are faced
with an absent, or rather, a hidden Lord. Like them we live in faith and
hope which are not rendered unambiguous by the problems of our
situation and our place in Christian history. Like them we face a time
when the Lord is rejected, when the irrelevance of the proclamation of
the risen Christ seems to the fore, and like them we have problems of
belief and unbelief which are not confined to those outside the believing
community. Like them, we find ourselves in a situation where thinking
about the faith is far from clear. We can begin to understand their

response and their searchings and let them illuminate our own situation and experience. Like them, when we look at the life of Jesus, we begin from the community's experience of the resurrection and work back. We too see each episode in the light of the whole event. We start from where we are and see Jesus in relation to that. The freedom we have found in him is reflected by the freedom we see in his life, and the stories about him justify our feeling of having been grasped by God and of having been overwhelmed by grace. Apart from our sharing in the resurrection, they can only be stories of the past, no more relevant than any other story of some past hero. Our experience – seen in the experience of the believing community – shapes the way we look at them, and in this we share in the attitudes of those who originally told and retold them.

There is a further point however. If the gospels are to be understood in the first instance, not as direct material for a recreation of the life of Jesus, but rather as witnesses of the early church to the significance they found in him, then due allowance must be given to the pre-understanding of that church which determined the way in which they approached the telling of his life. Their prior beliefs, their outlook, their understanding of the world, and their expectations all controlled the manner in which they pictured his life as it was lived on earth. Jesus is described in accordance with their overall understanding of him which is formed, not only as we have seen by their experience of him as the risen one in their midst, but also by their understanding of reality and of life in general.[6]

Again, in this the early church was not very different from us. I write this in the first week of Lent, a period in which most of us have accommodated the biblical story of the temptation of Jesus to our own understanding of reality. I told the story to a group of twelve year olds at the local school and I was taken to task by one lad for suggesting that Jesus was transported mentally rather than physically to the top of a high mountain to be shown 'all the kingdoms of the world and the glory of them'. My understanding of reality suggested that such an event was physically impossible and most of us would be prepared to see the lad's objection as based upon a prejudiced view of the gospels (in this case one formed by his elders) which resulted in a failure to understand the real significance of what was there before him. But then another lad asked me if I believed in a personal devil and I had to answer that, whilst most Christians, I thought, did, I along with many other Christians did not. My understanding of reality again made me feel that belief in a personal devil was not justified and I therefore believed that at this point also the biblical narrative was speaking pictorially rather than literally and factually. In principle, there is not any real difference between these two instances of interpretation of the biblical narrative. Our overall understanding of reality will make us include either one or both of them within the realm of imagery rather than of fact. And very few of us will be totally consistent.

Nearly all of us, if not indeed all of us, interpret the gospel narrative in the light of our understanding of reality and in the light of our acceptance of a belief that the early church described the life of Jesus from an outlook determined by their own world-view and by their expectations which followed from that. They described their understanding of Jesus' significance in the light of these and it is this fact which makes for problems for us since we can share neither their understanding of reality nor therefore their expectations. The gospels view Jesus through eyes accommodated to belief in a world which, depicted in terms of a three-tier universe, was invaded by visitors from both above and below. Angels came as messengers from the God who inhabited heaven whilst demons appeared as emissaries of the devil who dwelt below. The world was a battle-ground between the two opposing armies and man himself was pulled both ways as he was influenced by the forces of good and evil. The physical world itself, as well as its human inhabitants was putty in the hands of these supernatural beings.

The understanding of the early church, their 'life-world' – that is the assumptions they have about the structure of the world and of life in general and which therefore control their expectations and their beliefs in what is likely to happen – determined the way in which they saw and therefore told the stories about Jesus. Language is never simply descriptive. It is always interpretative for it sees any event through an outlook fashioned by particular assumptions. The description is never a photograph, but is a painting expressing a judgment upon what is described, and retailing its significance for the teller. What the gospels describe is determined, not only by what happened, but also by the outlook, the assumption, the beliefs, the understanding, and the expectations of the early community. Their 'world-view' caused them to describe Jesus in the way they did. More than that, it determined what they actually saw happen in his life. Our retelling of the events, our understanding of the significance of those events, must never forget this fact. They were truly men of their times, and we, in turn, have to be truly men of ours.

But, of course, the objection might be raised that certainty, that assurance provided by the gospels as traditionally understood is now threatened if not actually taken away. If Jesus is seen only as the early church was moved to remember him, could not their enthusiasm have taken over from their memory? Can we be sure that Jesus was such as to demand the early church's response and our allegiance? The answer is that we cannot be sure – or at least that the gospels themselves give us no incontrovertible proof that God was in Christ. Indeed, if the gospels describe Jesus in terms derived from the understanding of their age, there can be no guarantee that 'God' is not a concept to be assigned to the early stage of man's development. They cannot by themselves stand as a guarantee condemning the inadequacy of Laplace's 'I have no need of that hypothesis'. The gospels are a response of faith to the total event of Jesus, seen as the culmination of what was believed to be God's activity in the course of Jewish history. They encourage us to share in their faith, they can help us to see its resonableness, but that no other answer is possible to that history they cannot allow. 'These things are written that you might believe that Jesus is the Christ, the Son of God, and that believing you might have life in his name.' When John penned those words, he witnessed to a belief that Christians could walk only by faith and not by sight, and that his gospel could encourage response when it could not compel it. In the gospels we are invited to line ourselves up with the faith of the early church, to put ourselves under the judgment of its response, and to allow our own to be deepened, informed, and enriched thereby. This is what we preach through the gospels. And, really, what more should we be hoping for?

2

The Critics and the Gospels II:
The Synoptic Gospels

Whilst it is not at all obvious that familiarity must of necessity breed contempt, it is nevertheless certainly true that it can dull perception. Looking at familiar things, we can all too easily see what we are used to seeing so that in the end we see what we expect to see, and it is not until something unusual happens, until someone perhaps by their insights opens up our perspective in a new way, that what has been familiar to us is seen from a new angle and so goes on to take a new dimension which gives it a wholly new significance for us.

This is certainly true of our reading of the gospels. Our very familiarity with them means that all too often we do not see what is really there. At times it blunts their cutting edge, but also, and much more often, it accommodates them to our expectations. We assume that they are there primarily to give us facts about Jesus during his ministry and, assuming this, we tend to look at them through eyes determined by this expectation. Above all, we tend not to notice the differences between them, for these present awkward problems which we prefer to ignore. We play down the differences by suggesting that they are merely looking at Jesus from different angles, and we deny the real difficulties involved in harmonizing many of their accounts by suggesting that these very differences show that they are not telling an artificially unified story. The variations, we suggest, witness to the evangelists' truthfulness, to the fact that they are not giving us an artificially contrived account of what went on during the ministry of Jesus.

But it is really nowhere near as simple as that, for the differences are such that John's gospel cannot easily be brought into oneness with the rest to present a unified description of Jesus' ministry. More than that, the synoptic gospels themselves – those very gospels which we say look at Jesus from the same viewpoint to present a description and an understanding of his ministry which has a real common basis – even these place what are obviously the same event at different points in that ministry and report them in very different ways.

Perhaps one of the most important things for us who are preachers, and who want to preach the gospels as they really are, is to notice the differences and to use the gospels in such a way that our congregations should come to accept the true significance of them. We need to be more realistic – perhaps more honest – about the differences in the various gospels than in fact we are.[1]

Much recent gospel criticism has concerned itself with an effort to see what the evangelists were about when they wrote their gospels. It tries to understand the significance of the gospels as wholes. The starting point for a discussion of this question must be the simple fact that we have, not one gospel but four, that one of these, John, stands apart from the others in both much of its subject matter and in its manner of telling the life of Jesus, and that the other three, though having much in common, nevertheless differ in many significant ways. This particular method of looking at the gospels goes by the name of redaction criticism.[2]

Redaction criticism has three important things to say to us about the gospels. First, building upon the work of the source critics and all they did in an attempt to solve the synoptic problem – that is the problem caused by the fact that our first three gospels have both strong similarities and also very real differences – it tries to discover how these gospels were written. It tries to work out the way the evangelists set about their tasks for, if we can uncover this, if we can work out the mechanics of gospel writing, then we are likely to be in a better position for appreciating the reasons for their writing in the way that they did. The second contribution of redaction criticism is to help us to understand why the evangelists wrote as they did. What were their aims which caused them to write thus? What were the principles which determined the manner in which they told their story? If we can understand this, then we can go on to appreciate the redaction critic's third contribution which is to say something to us about the purpose of a gospel. It can unfold to us the significance of a gospel in general, and the reasons for the individual gospels in particular, and so can help us to understand more clearly how we should be using them.

First, then, what do the critics say about how the synoptic gospels were written? How did the evangelists go about their tasks? The problem here is to account not only for the similarities but also for the

differences between our first three gospels. They have a great number
of passages where not only their wording but also their settings in the
different gospels are almost exactly the same. On the other hand, they
also describe what are obviously the same events in different ways and
place them at different points in their gospels.[3] The similarities are such
that for the last fifty years or so it has been taken almost as axiomatic
that our first three gospels were linked in a direct literary relationship
and, after a consideration of all the possibilities this raised, the position
generally accepted has been that Mark was used as the primary source
of both Matthew and Luke.[4]

This position can account for the similarities between the gospels but
does it give an adequate explanation of the differences between them?
Can it, for instance, account for the fact that Matthew places together a
number of miracle stories which are, in Mark, scattered around the
gospel, or can it say why Luke's account of the rejection of Jesus by his
own countrymen at Nazareth is both in a different setting and of a
different kind from what is found in Mark? Some critics, feeling that it
cannot, have got away from the idea of some direct literary relationship between the three gospels to posit the belief in a gradual and
independent, though by no means isolated, parallel coming together of
various separate units both oral and written on a common outline of the
life of Jesus.[5] If this suggestion does away with the idea of long, written
sources a very different suggestion tries to account for the differences
between Mark and Luke by positing some lengthy written source, other
than Mark, as the main foundation of Luke's gospel.[6] Yet neither of
these positions can really account for the similarities between the three
gospels and so they have not commended themselves to the vast majority
of modern critics who continue to work on the supposition that Mark is
the primary source of both Matthew and Luke.

Matthew and Luke used Mark – this remains the best presupposition
from which to approach our first three gospels. They added to him, but
they also adapted him. The actual basis for these adaptations is not
easily discovered. Sometimes they appear to have altered Mark in order
to make him more explicitly the vehicle of their own beliefs whilst at
other times it is possible that they deserted him in favour of other,
parallel traditions which were to hand. Whatever the actual reasons for
the differences, however, the redaction critics tell us to take them seriously and they suggest that they will in fact give us a very real clue to
the nature and purpose of a gospel. Such an approach will enable us to
use the gospels rightly. We have to allow that Matthew and Luke used

Mark and then go on to ask why they differ from him as they do. What do the differences suggest about their purposes?

Their alterations cannot be accounted for on the supposition that they were in the cause of a more accurate presentation of the facts of Jesus' ministry. Luke has a much fuller account of the rejection of Jesus at Nazareth than has Mark. This, of course, could be because he had another source at his disposal which he preferred to use because of its additional information. That remains a possibility. More important, however, for us at the moment is the fact that he places the episode right at the beginning of his account of Jesus' ministry, rather than where it occurs in Mark's work at the end of the first stage of that ministry. Is this because Luke's other (hypothetical) source placed it here and that Luke decided that this was more accurate than Mark? This is hardly likely for both Luke's summary verses preceding the narrative itself and the inferences of Jesus' speech show that it could only have occurred after a fairly extensive ministry in Galilee. In other words, Mark's position is more likely to be right, and the reason for Luke's alteration is other than the cause of historical accuracy. His purpose in making Jesus' rejection at Nazareth the first of his scenes is to be found elsewhere than in the cause of accurate historical reconstruction.

The same approach can be seen in Matthew's alterations. Chapters eight and nine of his gospel contain a whole series of miracle stories which in Mark are scattered over the earlier stages of Jesus' ministry. In Matthew, on the other hand, they are strung together to give an increasing wonder at, and also increasing hostility to, Jesus as the bringer of the kingdom. Again, the reason is not historical accuracy, and when it is remembered that the miracles' collection is preceded by the teaching collection known as the Sermon on the Mount, then it must be suspected that both collections are equally the result of Matthew's systematizing. The parallel handling of word and of deed is intentional. As one recent commentator expresses it, 'He intends . . . to portray Jesus as the Messiah in Word and the Messiah in Deed.'[7]

If the alterations to Mark's order are not just in the cause of historical accuracy, those in the individual episodes cannot be accounted for simply in the cause of a better presentation – of a tidying up of Mark's loose descriptions and of his poor style. Though there are instances of this, it can only account for a small number of these alterations. Overall, the changes are far more decisive and significant. So, in Matthew, Mark's account of Peter's confession at Caesarea-Philippi – 'You are the

Christ' – becomes 'You are the Christ, the Son of the living God' whilst
Luke has 'You are the Christ of God'. The point is that each of these
confessions fits exactly into the particular evangelist's own understanding of Jesus. They do in fact further his proclamation of Jesus as he
understands him. Matthew has what is a developed understanding of
Jesus' significance, whilst Luke throughout sees Jesus as God's agent.
The same is true of their reporting of Jesus's response. In Mark there
is an abrupt turning aside of the acclamation in a command to silence.
In Luke this is even strengthened, but in Matthew, on the other hand,
it is omitted in favour of a total approval of Peter's response and he goes
on to talk about Peter's faith as the foundation and blueprint of the
church.

These variations reflect different theological outlooks on the part of
the different evangelists, and, because they fit completely into the overall outlook of the gospel in which they are set, it seems almost certain
that it was their different theologies which caused the evangelists to
report these incidents in the way that they did. In their hands, their
descriptions become expressions of their theology. Their alterations of
Mark are such as to make him a more ready vehicle of their own theological understanding of God's whole work in Jesus.

When the way in which Matthew and Luke handled Mark as a whole
is considered, it seems that they are revealed not merely as handers on of
the tradition that they received but also as revisers, adaptors, occasion-
ally censors and, perhaps even, creators of material. Their alterations
arise out of a definite point of view, from a particular way of looking at
Jesus, and, indeed, from a particular response they hope to get from
their readers. They are not in the nature of adjustments and improve-
ments, but are changes in outlook, expressions of different beliefs and
of different aims in the telling. In their hands Mark, though a respected
source, became subject to their own ideas and purposes, and he was
moulded by them to become a vehicle for their own theological beliefs
and insights. Nothing less than this is sufficient to describe the significance of their handling of him but, when this is accepted, it is possible
to make real sense of their alterations and really to come to grips with
what they were trying to do through them.

It is possible, however, to be rather more precise than this. In their
use of Mark, Matthew and Luke handled him with a kind of freedom
denied to copyists, collectors, and researchers, but which is of the stuff
of authors, commentators, and proclaimers. It is above all the manner
of the preacher who has his own message and distinctive point of view.

This supremely is what the evangelists are – visionaries and interpreters, urging others to 'see' Jesus as they 'saw' him, willing a particular response from those they were addressing. How often have we preachers in the pulpit retold a gospel episode in our own way – emphasizing details here, drawing out implications there – in order to make a point to our congregations, and how often have our descriptions been coloured and, indeed, controlled both by the significance of the event as we saw it, and by the response we were hoping to draw out from them? Sympathy, imagination, theological reflection, and the needs of those to whom we were preaching – all these played their part in the description of the event. By turning into living history what otherwise would have been just records, they enabled the past to address the present in a real and genuine way. In doing this we were doing precisely what Matthew and Luke had already done, and it seems likely therefore that Mark before them had been doing the same.

Such an estimate of Mark was not easily arrived at however. In the last century, once the priority of Mark was accepted, it was almost axiomatic that his gospel contained a clear, factual, and biographically controlled life of Jesus which the other evangelists had adapted – and so distorted – to serve their own particular ends. Mark's gospel was accepted as a true, accurate source for the life of Jesus.

This outlook had to give way, however, before a truer assessment of the facts. Not only does the way the early church handled the individual stories of the life of Jesus and the way the later evangelists handled Mark make it inherently unlikely that real biographical interest was the second evangelist's main concern, but a consideration of the Markan gospel itself makes it obvious that it wasn't. Mark just doesn't answer the questions that strict biographical interest would be concerned with asking. He tells us nothing of Jesus' early life, nothing about his appearance and family relationships, and little about his inner motives and understanding. Though he tells us that at his baptism Jesus saw the heavens opened, the Spirit descending, and heard a voice proclaiming his sonship, his account of the Temptation makes no attempt at all to show how Jesus worked out his response. Mark does not enable us to see how Jesus' ideas developed or how he entered upon the way of the cross. There is no attempt at all to get inside Jesus or to show what made him tick. It is written wholly from the external point of view of a disciple who is viewing events from a distance. From the point of view of biography he tells us nothing as to the reasons behind the agony in Gethsemane and the cry of desolation from the cross. The gospel as he penned it almost certainly ended at 16.8 and so contained no resurrection appearances at all. What biographer would have ended his story of Jesus with a message from a young man which was not passed on because 'they said nothing to anyone, for they were afraid'? Now, it is probably true that ancient biographical writing was not interested in chronological accuracy, in recreating the atmosphere of the past, or in the character development of the subject of the biography, and it may be true that there is more in common between the gospels and ancient biographical writing than has sometimes been allowed, but the essential points are not these but are to be found rather in the fact that the gospels do not provide material which satisfies our modern biographical concerns. Mark's material is highly selective and all could have occurred in a very short period of time. If we had only his gospel we would be unlikely to make Jesus' ministry extend for more than a year, and we would be quite ignorant of his age at its beginning. Mark's gospel describes a Galilean ministry followed by a Judaean ministry. Yet John's gospel allows for at least three visits to Jerusalem and some commentators would suggest that Matthew and Luke knew of more visits to the capital than the one Mark describes. If John is right and Mark is ignorant of these other visits (or more significantly if he chose simply to ignore them), it at once puts a question mark against his work as biography, but if one of the gospel records is determined by theological rather than by strictly biographical considerations, we cannot necessarily assume that it must have been John who was so influenced. On this, as on so many things, we can only answer that we do not know. We are just not able to say for certain whether Jesus made one or three visits to Jerusalem or whether his ministry lasted one or three years. These are questions which the gospels were not concerned to answer in the way we would like them answered, and it is likely that we moderns must accept that this difficulty runs right through their accounts of Jesus so that many of what are to us wholly legitimate interests have not the remotest chance of being satisfied.

We are now in a position to move on to consider the third point at which redaction criticism helps us to appreciate the gospels more fully. By helping us to understand how they were written and to appreciate why the authors wrote in the way they did, it can help us to understand the significance of a gospel and so to use it in a more effective way.

We have suggested that the evangelists were primarily theologians rather than historians, even though they were by no means indifferent to history for they were dealing with problems of a particular life in history, and with a belief that was expressed in time – the life of Jesus of Nazareth and the belief of early Christians that he was their Lord. They were also proclaimers rather than biographers, though again they were not indifferent to the life of Jesus for their message was built up in response to that life and was worked out to counter the problems that its ambiguities allowed constantly to come to the fore. Nevertheless, though not indifferent to history, they were going beyond history to draw out the significance that could be seen in that history to those who were prepared to look at it through the eyes of faith and in the belief that the subject of that life was now the living Lord. Above all they were drawing out the significance in that history for the present. They were interpreting it to their contemporaries. They were homing its lessons upon the lives and situations of those to whom they were writing.

For the evangelists were writing to real, particular people in concrete particular situations. They are best understood as preachers by way of the written word. They are, in fact, pastoral theologians. This is an insight that recent gospel criticism has brought out most strongly and it is a point of particular importance for us who would be preachers of the gospel through the gospels today.[8] It is just those times when we expound the gospels from our pulpits, when we are trying through them to allow the Word of God to run free in our congregations, when we are helping our listeners to be more open to the Living Lord – it is just these occasions when the intentions of the evangelists and our own most nearly coincide.

For the gospels bring the preaching of the early church to bear upon a particular situation. Behind each gospel lies the witness of the early church, but that witness is gathered up, moulded, and shaped by the vision of the individual author of the actual gospel. When Mark headed his work 'The beginning of the gospel of Jesus Christ, the Son of God' he was the first as far as we know to use the term 'gospel' of a written work. But in doing so he was linking his book up with the proclamation of the apostolic band. He is continuing to proclaim what Paul proclaimed when he spoke of 'my gospel' and so pointed not only to the link between his preaching and that of the church but also to his own insights, his own emphasis derived no doubt in large part from the situations which confronted him in his ministry. Even more important, Mark makes Jesus himself a proclaimer of the same message when, in his initial statement of Jesus' preaching, he says, 'Now after John was arrested, Jesus came into Galilee, preaching the Gospel of God, and saying, "The time is fulfilled, and the kingdom of God is at hand;

repent and believe in the Gospel." ' In this way therefore Mark states that his writing is a proclamation of the action of God in Jesus, that it is a call to respond to that action, and is itself an effective channel of God's approach to men.

But the gospel is now written down and is given in the form of a re-counting of incidents in the life of Jesus. Paul was not unconcerned with the life of Jesus and was certainly more interested in that life than some recent scholars have suggested. Nevertheless, he overall tells us little about Jesus and, somewhat more surprisingly, does not even appeal to that life when such an appeal would have provided him with powerful ammunition against his opponents. On the other hand, the gospels are completely concerned with that life. Can we account then for their out-look for, even though biographical interest as such was not their main concern, the life of Jesus was certainly the subject of their proclamation. Their belief in Jesus as Lord, and their understanding of his life had to be brought together.

The reason for this change of emphasis seems to have been, as we saw in the last chapter, the growing problems posed by continuing history. As history went on, belief in his Lordship was not made any easier by the failure of the parousia to occur, by the hostilities that believers had to face, and even by the tensions that appeared within the Christian community. All these caused the life of Jesus to be looked at in a new guise. The ambiguities of that life – the hiddenness of God's way in Jesus and the fact that he was crucified – came to the fore so that the Christian communities had to come to terms with them and to face both them and their own situations. The problems of the life of Jesus and the problems of their own living in the world had to be brought together and to be faced in the light of their belief in his Lordship.

For the redaction critics have taught us that the gospels are best understood when they are read as addressed to the early church itself rather than to those outside. Though evangelistic concerns are not to be excluded completely, these represent an interest which is subordinate to the internal concerns of the evangelist's own church. Our four gospels are appreciated best when they are seen as written for the early church as it struggled to understand more fully the real nature of what had happened and was continuing to happen in its midst and as it sought to work out its response to Jesus of Nazareth whom it now experienced as its risen Lord. The gospels are rooted in the lives of their particular churches as they draw upon their beliefs and respond to their needs.[9]

All this scholarly work can serve to make the gospels more useful tools for the parish priest as he tries to fulfil his ministry of the Word. How can we best make use of these insights?

First, as we saw in our last chapter, it is a question of our overall attitude, of the way in which we come to the gospels, of how we expect to be informed by them. We approach the evangelists as preachers; we sit at their feet to hear their proclamation. And we approach them as pastors as we listen into, as we overhear their concerns for their contemporaries. We have got used to eavesdropping on Paul as he exercises his pastoral ministry to his churches (though, alas, it must be admitted that we do not always acknowledge this in our treatment of him) and modern scholarly study of the gospels suggests that we should also be looking at the evangelists' work in the same way, that we should be treating their writings as their testimony, their witness to the Lord in whom they believed and whom they hoped to commend the more to their readers.[10] The first questions we should be asking are, What is the evangelist seeking to proclaim to his contemporaries through his use of this episode in the life of Jesus? How is he seeking to strengthen their faith by way of it? What insights into belief in the Lord Jesus does it give? We accept them as preachers and pastors and we view their writings as their testimony to their living Lord.

Now, as we have said before, this does not mean that we cannot use their witness as a source of insight into the life of Jesus. Such a search is neither impossible nor illegitimate. It is, however, difficult, for the gospels do not give us a direct entry into that life. Information about the life of Jesus, though not incidental, has nevertheless to be gleaned. The real harvest is the evangelists' proclamation. So, for instance, let us assume that we are to preach on August 6, upon the Transfiguration of Jesus. As an incident in the life of Jesus, how are we to understand it – as having an effect upon him or upon the disciples, or upon both? Are we to preach it as an expression of divine approval upon his decision to go to the cross? The fact that the heavenly visitors are with him suggests this, yet the divine voice implies a message, not to him, but to the apostles. Yet as a witness to the apostles it is singularly limited for they are told to tell no one until after the resurrection from the dead, and they are completely lacking in any kind of perception. As a 'disclosure situation' it is singularly inept.

But the way the evangelists handle the story suggests that such a historical throw-back was not their primary concern. The present is their interest and their aim is to allow the story to serve as a disclosure to their contemporaries who are to stand on the mount, to have a momentary glimpse of their Lord in glory, to learn from the incomprehension of the disciples, and to come down from the mount with a lasting memory of its lessons. So Mark, followed by Matthew, sees the event as pointing forward to the parousia, as a moment of anticipation of what one day will be fully revealed when the suffering will be transformed into glory. Luke, on the other hand, through his talk about the Jerusalem exodus, pictures the scene in terms of the ascension which he alone describes. Luke's readers are to look, not forward, but back to share in the value judgment on Jesus which the ascension proclaims. For all the evangelists, the moment is a glimpse of reality in the midst of the hiddenness of the way of the cross; it is a challenge to their readers to continue to read what they are to go on to tell against its true backcloth, and then to let that same backcloth set the real import upon their own pilgrimage. The evangelists through their gospels address their readers directly. We are to listen in, to let their proclamation become a means of disclosure to us. We do it, not by a historical reconstruction of the life of Jesus, but by an appreciation of their insights, of their address.

But Mark and Luke are not using the episode in the same way. Their insights have to be sought out. Their descriptions have to be teased, to be approached with sympathy and imagination. And one of the most informative ways in which this is done is with the aid of a synopsis, which must be one of our most important tools in our efforts to take the evangelists seriously.[11]

In the preparation of our sermons, a synopsis will be a constant aid for, by comparing how an event in the life of Jesus is variously described by the different evangelists, we will be able, not only to see the nature of its basis in the life of Jesus, but, more important for our immediate purpose, to throw light upon the purpose of the evangelists in their recounting of it. To pass from one evangelist to another in this way is not only to have all of them opened up, but also to be made more open to their concerns.

But, if we are to see the evangelists in the light of each other, we are also to see the individual episodes in the light of the whole gospel in which they are set. There is to be an interplay between the particular episode and the gospel taken as a whole, for the gospels are careful constructions which make out a unified case for believing in Jesus. When Luke penned his introduction to his two volumes he was, in classical terms and in the manner of his best contemporaries, maintaining his concern to compose a work which was carefully researched and delicately constructed. On first sight, his prologue suggests a concern to write an accurate historical narrative, but further consideration of his work soon suggests that this was not his main aim. Had it been, the results would have shown him to have been singularly inept both in the gospel and in Acts. However, when he expressed his desire to write an 'orderly account' he was referring rather to a step by step unfolding of a thesis, a carefully constructed presentation of a case, in this instance of that for the Lordship of Jesus. Each incident adds to the whole and is to be seen in the light of the whole.

And so our second necessary tool for the preparation of our sermons must be those commentaries which take into account recent scholarly work and which try to take the theologies of the evangelists seriously.[12] The overall theological beliefs, the overall convictions of the particular evangelist must be considered and the contribution of the particular passage must be uncovered in the light of this.

For a theological approach to the evangelists needs to be conscious of two angles. There is, first, that which concerns itself with how the particular evangelist approaches the great theological themes of Christianity – of his understanding of the person of Jesus, of his approach to the cross, the Holy Spirit, to the Jews, to the Gentiles, and so on. This concern with the evangelist's outlook, with his slant, with his emphasis is by no means new and would have found a place in all the commentaries over the years. Now, however, there is a second angle, and this is concerned with the overall structure of his book, with his approach to Christianity as a whole, and with his total understanding of the whole nature of God's work in Jesus. He is now seen as a much more creative exponent of the total significance of Christianity, and his theology is to be found, not merely in particular slants and emphases at the edge of his narrative, but is to be seen through the whole shape of the narrative, the nature of what is included, and the entire presentation of the work. This is a much more radical approach for it sees the whole gospel as determined by and as expressive of the evangelist's beliefs. The theology of the evangelists is no longer seen as an additional layer – an added extra – in their gospels, but is accepted as the fundamental factor, not merely in determining the emphases and individual characteristics of their writings, but also in controlling their whole shape, outlook and purpose.[13]

Our preaching therefore will always be concerned with the situation of the evangelist and of the community to whom he writes and will bring out our understanding of him as a pastor. Now here, of course, there is a difficulty, for the evangelists do not tell us directly of the situation before them. It has to be inferred from their gospels and there is obviously the problem of circularity here. However, the danger cannot be sidestepped but is inherent in the very nature of our documents.

So we will use sympathy and a controlled imagination in an effort to recreate the circumstances of the evangelist and his readers. Mark's gospel will be preached as born out of the sufferings of those to whom it is addressed. There is much to commend the traditional view that it was written for the church in Rome after the death of many of her earliest leaders during the persecution of Nero. The church undergoes suffering and waits almost desperately for the appearing of the Lord. Matthew's situation, on the other hand, is much more settled. That gospel shows all the marks of a community production, of a church that is reasonably securely established, which, though linked closely by belief and racial ties to the Jewish people, is open to the mission to the Gentiles. Though reasonably well-established, it is not without internal tensions and these are probably heightened by something of the nature of a running battle in which it is engaged with the Jewish synagogue which is established nearby. It no longer looks anxiously for the parousia, though it continues to believe in it. When it comes it will bring judgment to the church as well as to the world. Luke is conscious of the passing of time since the life of the Lord. The failure of the parousia to happen has produced something like a failure of nerve and Luke seeks to counter this by emphasizing the reality of the Lordship of Jesus which was established at the ascension and by showing how the life of Jesus fulfilled at all significant points the expectations of the scriptures as it also brought God's saving action in the Jewish people to a climax. Luke is concerned by the failure of the Jewish people as a whole to respond, for he himself, though a Gentile by race, seems to have found the beginnings of salvation in the Jewish community. He is perhaps best understood as a Godfearer who sees Christianity as the completion and crown of the initial covenant with Abraham.

There is, of course a danger in this approach and the preacher is as open to its enticements as is the gospel critic himself. Overall, the biggest pit-fall arises from the fact that it is all too easy to be carried away, to let our own ideas become dominant, to take off on our own, to let our imagination run away with us. Our preaching then becomes subject to ourselves, and our gospel preaching is taken over by that expression of our own opinions and enthusiasms that it is meant to safeguard against.[14]

Using the legitimate and wholly desirable method of redaction criticism in the pulpit can lead us into an approach where we are controlling the gospels and reading into them rather than reading out of them and letting them control us. This criticism has often been levelled at the redaction critic and, it must be confessed, it can be justified, for redaction criticism like any other method of interpreting the gospels, can easily become over-subjective.

For the fact is of course that we cannot be completely objective. It is well that both the scholar and the preacher should be aware of this from the beginning. It will make for honesty and humility in their approach, and the preacher should not confuse these with hesitancy or with failure to give a lead to the congregation. He will enter into dialogue with the gospels and, if he is wise, he will pursue the approach of any good teacher and enter into dialogue with his congregation. The fact that they are silent does not mean that their participation in the sermon should be wholly passive or that they should be seen as empty vessels waiting to be filled with the preacher's own words of wisdom. Again, the preacher will recognize the difference between the gospel situation and his own. He will not try to extract ready-made answers from them. He will approach the gospels with a controlled freedom brought about by an element of dialogue between himself and them.

One further point must be added about this way of approaching the gospels in our sermons. Modern study accepts the distinctiveness of outlook of the individual gospel writers. When Matthew and Luke wrote their second editions of Mark, they were not just enlarging and supplementing their predecessor's work. As we have seen, they were revisers of it, and their revisions are to be seen very much as adaptations and modifications. They were meant to displace Mark – at least so far as the people for whom they wrote were concerned. They were meant to stand on their own and to be read on their own terms both historically and theologically. Matthew not only revised Mark's seemingly poor opinion of the disciples, he reshaped certain aspects of Mark's presentation of Jesus. We have already seen how he exalts Jesus' person at Caesarea Philippi and at the Transfiguration. He corrects Mark at points where it would seem the earlier gospel would make Jesus hostile to the law. Luke has a different understanding of the cross from that found in Mark. He denies Jesus' dealings with Gentiles during the ministry, and limits Jesus' resurrection appearances to the area of Jerusalem.

It seems therefore that if we are to understand the gospels correctly, and to take hold of the message being proclaimed through them, we should approach each one as an individual work to be read in the first instance apart from the others and to be interpreted in terms of itself alone.[15] Each has a distinctive presentation of the history of Jesus. One gospel's account of any particular happening should not be read in terms of what is found in one of the others. To do so can only and often distort the individual gospel's message. So, for instance, because Luke's gospel contains an account of the ascension, the final episode of Matthew's work should not be read as its equivalent or in its terms. Matthew's concern and his understanding of the mode of the Lord's presence in the world is very different from Luke's and an ascension event as such appears to play no part in his theology. Nor should an event described in one gospel necessarily be seen as a prelude (or as a sequence for that matter) to an event recorded in another. Violence can only be done to both accounts if attempts are made to harmonize John's description of the bestowal of the Spirit with that given at Pentecost. To try to do so not only makes for an impossible position in the days of the early church, but also turns attention aside from what the evangelists are really trying to say through their individual stories.

Perhaps nowhere is the difficulty of harmonization, and the blunting of the individual evangelist's message that so often follows from it, better seen than in the account of Jesus on the cross and the treatment of his words from it. We tend to treat John's 'I thirst' in terms of Mark's 'My God, my God, why hast thou forsaken me' which itself we view against John's 'It is finished' which we then see as a prelude to Luke's 'Father into thy hands I commend my spirit'. But, to do so blunts the proclamation that the evangelists are trying to make. Matthew/Mark, Luke, and John paint in the words of Bornkamm 'three great, and in themselves profoundly different, pictures of the crucified. They must not be taken as fragments of a historical record and then pieced together to make a whole, however clearly all of them express in their differences and despite their differences, the mystery of the person, mission, and death of Jesus'.[16] When they are taken together and are harmonized into one historical record, the significance of the individual word as that particular evangelist saw it is inevitably reduced, for the awfulness of the word of desolation is mellowed by the word of triumph, and the word of forgiveness is almost inevitably wrongly directed. There can be little more wrong interpretation than the significance given to John's final word in Stainer's 'Crucifixion'. But, if the gospels are taken together and not treated on their own terms, this is bound to happen. There is much to be said for the preacher's confining his attention during the Three Hours' service on Good Friday to *one* of the Four Gospels, and not passing from one to another, or attempting to harmonize one with another.[17] No doubt we must bring together, albeit in some form of creative tension, the insights of a Mark, a Luke, and a John, but these cannot just be rolled into one picture as a single history and theology of the cross. The depth of the insight of each particular evangelist must first be fathomed and tried out for what it is. Otherwise, we shall remain in shallow waters indeed.

For their theology cannot just be harmonized in the interests either of our own beliefs or of later theories of what is right doctrine. No one of them can be treated as expressing the whole understanding of later orthodoxy. We shall therefore not try to bring them together into an artificial harmony or to give them a perfection which is not theirs.

So, in our sermons we shall try to let the evangelists speak for themselves. Our aim will be to hear what they were really saying at a particular moment in time. That is as far as the redaction critic can take us, but to go along with him would seem to be an absolute necessity if we are to begin to hear the message of the gospels aright. What may begin as a chore can soon take on the character of a pilgrimage and its goal can be real insight and understanding.

Its value, however, is not easily discovered for it allows for no instant relevance. It will not necessarily let us pass straight from the past to the present in one easy movement. Its result is to see the gospels very much as documents from their own times and to uncover the evangelists as first-century men. Indeed, its immediate result may seem to be to remove them from us, to distance them from our own time. Having learnt what a particular passage meant then may not help us into an easy entry into what it can mean now. The temptation is always to try to pass too easily from the 'then' to the 'now', for such a quick transition usually means either a wrenching of the original so that it becomes damaged, perhaps beyond repair in the process, or it makes for something superficial in the present, or it works rather like the conjuror's sleight of hand which, though awaking admiration, leaves the viewer puzzled rather than convinced. The gospel critic warns us that there are no short cuts, and we as preachers would do well to heed his warning.

3

The Critics and the Gospels III:
The Fourth Gospel

William Temple called the Fourth Gospel the 'profoundest of all writings'[1] and few works have succeeded better at making something of that profundity available to a wide circle than did his own *Readings in St John's Gospel*. In his introduction he wrote, 'I am chiefly concerned with what arises in my mind and spirit as I read: and I hope that this is not totally different from saying that I am concerned with what the Holy Spirit says to me through the Gospel.'

Yet Temple's work was not uninterested in those questions which engage the critics. Though he maintained that it was not primarily concerned with 'what the writer consciously intended' nor with the question of how much of the contents of the gospel had 'its origin in the deeds and words of the Lord Jesus when on earth', he does in fact base his own insights on his understanding of the evangelist's actual proclamation and devotes the major part of his not insubstantial introduction to the question of the historicity of the sayings and of the validity of the Johannine portrait of the Christ.

These are the fundamental questions which concern the critics. And the important point as far as the Fourth Gospel is concerned is the recognition that the critics' debate arises, not from some perverse delight or from some obscurantist concern, but from issues which the gospel itself raises so unmistakeably.

For the most obvious fact about the Fourth Gospel and the one which absolutely necessitates the critical discussion is that it is different. To pass over to it from the synoptics is to enter almost another world where, though the leading figures remain the same and the overall events follow a recognizable path, there is a distinctiveness, a newness, an otherness about its presentation. Familiar characters are bathed in a new light, seen from a new angle; they talk in a strange, unfamiliar language, employing new images and expressing new ideas. The evangelist proclaims a message that is distinct, far from wholly other than that found in the synoptists, but strangely transposed, refurbished, reshaped. And the reader will find new stirrings inside himself. For some they will be ones of release, of fulfilment, of comprehension, as the Fourth Gospel clarifies what they have begun to understand of Jesus, as it illuminates their response and makes sense of their strivings. For others, it will retain its strangeness; they will remain slightly uneasy, never feeling completely at home in its pages, never quite on the same wave-length, never entirely at one with its proclamation. All, however, will be moved by it as they seek to come to terms with it. Such is its greatness and its power.

That it stands apart – alone – is clear. In the first place, its manner, its style, is so different. It is indeed wholly other than that of the synoptics. Their circumscribed, easily detachable episodes have given way to expanded narratives, and their collections of short, though related, sayings have passed into lengthy discourses where the dominant theme is developed through literary devices which, using ambiguity, irony, misunderstanding and restatement ensure a clarification which makes for a better understanding of the original. The whole work has a dramatic unity about it which allows a clear, but elusive, picture to emerge. John was an artist of no mean calibre.

And then, again, the matter is different. Like the synoptics, John's account of the ministry begins with John the Baptist and draws to a conclusion with an entry in triumph into Jerusalem. A turning point again occurs around the narrative of the Feeding of the Five Thousand which, as in Mark, is followed by a voyage of the disciples across the sea and the coming to them of Jesus when he walks across the water. A confession by Peter follows soon after. Otherwise, things are very different. In place of the synoptics' single journey to Jerusalem, John records at least three visits there. Jesus cleanses the Temple at the beginning of the ministry, and his final stay in Jerusalem is extended far beyond the short visit allowed for in the other three gospels. His ministry overlaps that of John the Baptist and enables some of the Baptist's disciples to transfer from John to him. The Last Supper occurs a day earlier than in the synoptics so that Jesus, after carrying his own cross to the place of execution, dies upon the cross as the passover lambs are being slain. There is no trial before Caiaphas and the Sanhedrin but only a preliminary interrogation before Annas.

And the response to Jesus is different. From the beginning he is recognized completely for what he is. In the very first chapter, John the Baptist acknowledges him as the 'Lamb of God who takes away the sin of the world' and proclaims, 'I have seen and have borne witness that this is the Son of God.' Disciples acknowledge him as the Messiah, the one 'of whom Moses in the Law and the Prophets wrote', the Son of God who is King of Israel. Mary his mother has absolute trust in him. The Samaritans accept him as Saviour of the World.

But the greatest difference is found in Jesus himself. Quite apart from its style, the content of his message is very unlike what is given in the synoptic gospels. No longer does Jesus proclaim the nearness of the kingdom of God and call for repentance in the face of its coming. Indeed, the kingdom is mentioned only twice, and Jesus gives no teaching either about its present existence or its future manifestation. Whilst it is not true that the Johannine Jesus has departed completely from apocalyptic terminology, for the future resurrection at the last day is retained, it no longer provides the framework for his teaching. John's Jesus describes himself as Son of Man but he is no apocalyptic figure appearing at the last day, nor does the term express the necessity of suffering in the simple synoptic form. The Son of Man descends and ascends, is lifted up and glorified through death. He gives his disciples the true-food which is his flesh and blood. He is the mediator between God and man who has come down from heaven and who is glorified through his exaltation upon the cross. Jesus no longer talks of suffering as something that he must undergo, as something unwelcome but entered upon determinedly for the sake of his vocation. It now becomes his glorification, and the glory both relieves the suffering and also cushions Jesus from it. So there is no Gethsemane, no struggling with fear before the unsought pain, no cry of desolation from the cross. John's Jesus comes out to meet his captors, he determines his own path along which he carries his own cross and he dies with a cry of triumph upon his lips. No centurion makes his acknowledgment at this point for Jesus himself has made his own witness crystal clear.

For in John Jesus has all the time pointed to himself with an openness and directness which is very different from the indirect christological witness of the synoptics. Here is no hidden figure, expressing an ambiguous authority, whose otherness has to be drawn out and evaluated, to be uncovered and assessed, but an open manifestation of authority, backed by unique claims. Jesus constantly and unambiguously proclaims himself as the only divine saviour of universal hope and expectation. 'I, when I am lifted up from the earth will draw all men to myself'. So Jesus explains himself in symbols having an Old Testament basis but capable of a universal significance. He is the 'bread of life', the 'light of the world', the door to salvation, the 'resurrection and the life', the 'true vine', the 'good shepherd'. In the Fourth Gospel Jesus proclaims, not the kingdom, but himself. The synoptic proclaimer of good news has become the proclaimed arbiter of salvation.

And so in John the miracles take on a new significance. They are no longer marks of compassion granted as a result of faith (which, in fact, is really little more than a cry for help) on the part of the afflicted, and witnessing indirectly to the fact of Jesus' link with the kingdom, but are now entered into primarily as signs of the reality of Jesus' own status and work. The balance has altered. Compassion takes a lower place; the significance is all important. At Cana John sees, not a caring Lord, but one giving a prefiguration of his saving work; at Bethany, though Jesus weeps, it is only the Jews who associate his emotion with love; the evangelist probably intends a real distress which amounts to anger, either at unbelief, or in the presence of physical death. That the emotion is not compassion is suggested by the fact that Jesus had earlier deliberately held back; his act of power had to be nothing less than a raising from the dead.

So the differences are great indeed, and it is probably only our very familiarity with John's gospel and our long-maintained attitude of uncritical harmonization which dulls our awareness of its otherness and lets us read it through eyes which make it conform to the synoptic pattern. But this is to reduce the Fourth Gospel and to dull its witness to Jesus. Real appreciation of its testimony must let us take full account of these differences.

What though is their significance? This is a question which must concern every interpreter of the Fourth Gospel be he the parish priest in his role as preacher or the academic when he dons the mantle of commentator. That the question is of more than academic concern is confirmed by the fact that the right answer will not only establish a legitimate way of using John's work, but will also have much to say about the person of Jesus and the making of an adequate and legitimate understanding of him.

The critics of the earlier decades of this century tended to stress the differences between John and the synoptics and to make the significance of them very great indeed. They suggested that the Fourth Gospel was far removed both from the person of Jesus of Nazareth and from the main-stream of early Christianity. It was suggested that it could offer little information about Jesus as he was and that its interpretation of him was made in the light of external religious influences derived from Hellenistic or Gnostic sources. It was thought to be late, having little direct contact with Palestine or with traditions going back to the time of the earliest Christian community, and having little or no connection with the apostle John.

Such an estimate was plainly out of step with the general use of the Fourth Gospel in the church at large and had little in common with the value that was put upon it by the vast majority of its users. The church at large found that it made Jesus available to them in a profound and legitimate way. It refused to be put off by the critics and quite simply sat tight and waited for them to catch up!

And the critics did move on from their earlier negative handling of John's work to come round to a much more positive appreciation of it. The Fourth Gospel is now seen to be earlier than often used to be propounded, and recent textual discoveries mean that it can be dated before the end of the first century. It is now possible to see it as based upon a tradition which, even if not actually going back to John, claims to have John as its mentor and ultimate source. For that tradition can now be seen as owing more to a sectarian form of Judaism which flourished at the time of Jesus than to Hellenistic or Gnostic sources. Archaeological evidence now suggests that the Fourth Gospel reveals some accurate knowledge of Jerusalem at the time of Jesus, whilst recent literary work on the gospel itself makes it likely that genuine sayings of Jesus of a synoptic kind and sometimes of a parabolic type lie at the basis of many of the discourses.[2]

All this is gain because it narrows the gap between the Fourth Gospel and that compelling figure in Palestine whose ministry, death, and resurrection set in motion that apprehension which John's gospel so brilliantly conveys. Nevertheless, too much should not be claimed for these new discoveries nor for the results of these new insights. The gap between Jesus of Nazareth and Jesus as he appears in the Fourth Gospel has been narrowed rather than bridged. One cannot pass from one to the other without a jump made possible by the springboard of Easter and the faith of the early church. That is true as we have seen of all the gospels, but that the gap is wider and the necessary jump longer in the Fourth Gospel than in the others remains certain. The differences between John and his synoptic cousins make this judgment inevitable. And it should not be forgotten that even such a conservative interpreter as William Temple recognized that there was more than the witness of

Jesus to himself recorded in the sayings of the Fourth Gospel. His solution was to see its discourses as legitimate extensions which unfolded what by implication was contained in the actual sayings of Jesus. So he maintained that Jesus could well have said, 'I am the true vine' and the elaboration of that statement in such sayings as 'Apart from me ye can do nothing', though a legitimate extension, nevertheless 'is a record as much of the disciples' experience as of the Lord's utterance.'[3]

Temple here points the way to a true appreciation of the significance of the Fourth Gospel for us. Like all the gospels, it contains more than a record of Jesus as he was during his time on earth. Like the synoptic gospels, John looks at Jesus with a vision which has been enlarged by the experience, life, and faith of the early church. The Jesus of history is described in terms of the Lord they know him now to be. That, as we have seen, is true of all the gospels so that John should not be completely separated off from them.

Nevertheless John does present a very different picture of Jesus from the one that is to be found in the synoptic gospels. Jesus as the Fourth Gospel presents him is always aware of his status, of his eternal relationship with the Father, of his coming from God and his going to God, and of his total unity with God in a way which is just not verbalized and made explicit by the Jesus of the other gospels. John draws out, clarifies, and makes plain what in them is hidden and only latent. Statements of Jesus like 'I and the Father are one', 'He that has seen me has seen the Father', and 'Before Abraham was I am' go far beyond what is found in the synoptic gospels to conceptualize and express what in them remains at most both unarticulated and indirect.

The greatness of John's response – the depth of his insight and the genius of his apprehension – inevitably means that the past becomes more transparent to its significance so that it is caught up more fully into the present. The present is slotted over the past so that the two cohere in a single whole. He begins with the flesh as he begins with the past but the flesh and the Word, the present and the past, are brought together and, inevitably, the lesser is caught up in the greater. John's gospel is a profound interpretation of Jesus as he was known in and through the life of the believing community which, brought into being by his life, death, and resurrection, responded to him in faith and looked back at his life to describe it as the life of the Lord they knew him now to be.[4]

Because the background of John's gospel is different from that of the synoptics, his understanding of Jesus is different from theirs. Different presuppositions shape the different presentations of Jesus as these reflect different understandings of his significance.

We therefore use John most realistically when we see his gospel as a profound testimony to the whole event of Jesus given by a particular community which had discovered light and life through his name. We learn from their reponse and try to use it to allow the risen Lord to address us now. It is an inspired meditation which confronts the present through narratives set in the past, for its subject is none other than the living Lord as he meets one part of the church which has been brought into being by him.

The form of the gospel itself eases us into this approach. Running through it all is a fine sense of drama which causes both its discourses and its narratives to be unfolded in a dramatic manner. The signs are nearly all 'extended' in one way or another to bring out the significance which John found in them. The introductory sign – that of changing water into wine at Cana of Galilee – is closely associated with the story of the cleansing of the Temple in Jerusalem to enable both episodes to point out the finality of Jesus in contrast to the transitoriness of the old dispensation's approach to God. The other signs unfold the significance of Jesus and they are carefully selected and orchestrated to come to a climax in that of the raising of Lazarus which both makes clear the full nature of Jesus' achievement and which, by being the immediate cause of the Passion, also introduces the means by which the achievement is itself accomplished.

The discourses, likewise, are constructed with a careful eye which enables them to move forward, though not directly, nevertheless inevitably, to a climax. Dramatic aids are employed to the full. A statement which itself has the mark of irony in so far as it is tantalizingly capable of being understood at more than one level, is followed by misunderstanding which leads to a further unfolding of the original statement in such a way as to draw out its deepest meaning. So in chapter 3, Jesus is made to say, 'Truly, truly, I say to you, unless one is born of water and the Spirit, he cannot enter the kingdom of God.' Nicodemus patently misunderstands Jesus, but the misunderstanding enables the true meaning of the saying to be drawn out so that the discourse becomes a highly significant witness to the reality of Jesus. That the discourse as a whole is a composition of the evangelist is further suggested by the fact that it is quite impossible to say where the statement of Jesus is supposed to end and the comments of the evangelist to begin. The one passes imperceptibly into the other in such a way as to show that no real distinction can be made between them.

Recent commentators have frequently suggested that parts at least of John's gospel began life as homilies addressed to the congregation when it was gathered together to celebrate the eucharist.[5] Much of the gospel can be approached as sermons given to the Christian community in order to strengthen its faith, to help it to enter more fully into the mystery of Christ, and to enable it to withstand the attacks of objectors. Though the sign is not always connected very closely with the discourse that follows, it serves as an introduction, as a spring-board, for the discourse which appears to be based upon what is virtually a text which follows on from the sign and is the point of departure for the actual discourse.

Preaching from the discourses is not easy and it is certainly much more difficult than it is from the teaching of Jesus as it is given in the synoptic gospels. And the reason is precisely the fact that they are already preached – that they are already in the form of a profound meditation which is in itself a form of art and which already makes its own point with telling directness and precision. It unfolds the real significance of Jesus in a singularly profound and telling way. All we can do – perhaps all we need to do – is to clarify the meaning for our congregations, to explain its terms, to set it against its background and so to draw out its imagery, to help our congregations to see the development of its ideas and the movement of its thought.

What we do in reality is to give an exposition of it which opens out its meaning. Translation of its insights, however, is not made easier by the fact that many of them are expressed in the context of a bitter disputation with the Jews. Indeed, it is sometimes suggested that the whole gospel is constructed in the form of a trial in which the Father, the Spirit, John the Baptist, the scriptures, and, not least, his own works witness to the truth of Jesus and against the Jews who are set in the role of his unyielding opponents.[6] Jesus makes his own witness to them plainly. In contrast to the synoptists, John makes Jesus openly transgress the Sabbath, and unambiguously make blasphemous claims.

This form of the gospel – its dramatic, searching, climatic witness to Jesus – accounts for the extremely controversial nature of the Johannine Lord who meets his opponents in a head-on clash and who in this exhibits qualities which are not always attractive. It gives the gospel a parochial atmosphere of one particular time and place which exists alongside its transcendence, and makes for a certain contradictory 'feel' to the work as a whole. His gospel was written at a time when the break between Christians and Jews was being finalized. Alongside the immediacy of the appeal of many of its discourses therefore there is also that which sets it in the middle of first-century controversies and which tends to distance it from us. Our task as preachers is to enable its timelessness to run free by so unfolding its imagery and so explaining its first-century setting that it is enabled to address our listeners the more effectively. We have to help it to transcend its setting. We have to try to resist the temptation to preach from a text which we use as a starting-off point for thoughts which are apart from the gospel itself. Rather, we have to let the passage as a whole in the context of the total gospel's understanding, make its witness to the risen, contemporary, Lord.

The same is true of our preaching of John's narratives. They are signs which witness to the nature and significance of Jesus and it is as such that they invite us to use our own imagination, insights, and interpretative skill to enter into John's thoughts and to establish a real measure of empathy with him. They invite our imagination and our meditation, and we preach them in such a way as to encourage our congregations to employ their own insights and understanding. In this way we can follow up Temple's concern with 'what arises in my mind and spirit when I read'. That John himself would have encouraged this manner of interpreting his work seems certain from his own insistence that 'it is the Spirit which quickeneth, the flesh profiteth nothing'. and by his reporting the Lord as promising the gift of the Spirit who will 'take of mine and declare it unto you'. If these sayings give an insight into his understanding of the nature of his own work, they inevitably invite his readers to enter upon their own act of interpretation.

And this way of reading John's stories does give value to those points which, if the narratives are taken as historical reports, can only perplex and confuse the reader. An instance of this is found in John's story of the raising of Lazarus. As a piece of factual reporting, the evangelist's comment in verses 5 and 6 of chapter 11 – 'Now Jesus loved Martha and her sister and Lazarus. So when he heard that he was ill, he stayed two days longer in the place where he was' – at least seems to be a non sequitur of massive proportions. At worst, it is thoroughly perplexing for it suggests a using of Lazarus which does not refrain from allowing him the trauma of physical death. But, of course, this is not the level at which John means it to be understood. Such an approach can do nothing to uncover the ideas or feelings of the earthly Jesus. John here is engaged in interpretation and he is describing what are presented as temporal events *sub specie aeternitatis*. Indeed little of the facts of history can be uncovered from the narrative as a whole. It is better to leave the level of historicity aside entirely and to direct all attention to significance.

When this is done, the story takes on a profound meaning and it preaches Jesus in a dramatic and all-embracing way. Lazarus must die because to seek anything less than eternal life from Jesus – to find in him something else, to let him satisfy any other need – is to deny both his real value and his real gift. It is ultimately to use him, to seek to sub-ordinate him and so to make him less than Lord and God. And Lazarus must die, because acceptance of Jesus inevitably means the death of the old and the birth of the new. To Nicodemus Jesus had said, 'You must be born again' and here in Lazarus that challenge is dramatically spelt out. So teaching on the meaning of Jesus, of his gift, and of his person is given to Martha and the interview reaches its climax in the confession of faith, 'Yes Lord: I believe that you are the Christ, the Son of God, he who is coming into the world.'

Martha fetches Mary who has not come to the level of Martha's faith. Mary repeats Matha's original complaint and her weeping causes Jesus to be deeply moved in the face of unbelief and of death. They go to the tomb and here even Martha's earlier faith appears to let her down. How-ever, it becomes the occasion for Jesus' prayer and for his promise that through him they would see the glory of God. And so there comes the striking climax, 'Lazarus, come out'. The dead man comes, still bound in bandages, still therefore in the grip of death. This provokes Jesus' further command, 'Unbind him, and let him go'. Here is the dramatic conclusion, but it also presents the theological climax of the narrative. Lazarus will still die. He must, once again sooner or later, go through that death which is the lot of every man. But its character has changed completely. He has already died in Christ. In Christ he has already passed through death to life. Death no longer holds him in its clutches. Into his state of being hemmed in by death and all that it represents comes the call of Christ, and when that call finds a response in man, then is heard the further call which becomes both a promise and a gift, 'Loose him and let him go'. So, in dramatic form, is proclaimed what Jesus himself has earlier been made to say, 'I am come that they might have life . . . Every one who believes in me has passed from death to life.'

But the life of Lazarus leads directly and inevitably to the death of Jesus. Because Lazarus lives, Jesus dies: and conversely, only because Jesus dies does Lazarus live. The raising of Lazarus becomes the immediate grounds for the Council's decision to go at once for the death of Jesus. Jesus is no longer to escape from the hand of his enemies as he has done so many times before for his hour has now come. That which the dramatic episode of the raising of Lazarus has illustrated and which is to be accomplished only through the death of Jesus is now to be effected. Jesus is to be glorified through his own death which is to be the means of mankind's coming to life. In what is probably the supreme example of John's irony, the evangelist has the High Priest himself acknowledge that 'Jesus should die for the nation, and not for the nation only, but to gather into one the children of God who are scattered abroad'. The drama of the gospel is now set to move forward to its climax.

John's work, then, is a profound interpretation which presents us with the Living Lord as the Johannine community has discovered him and as it has been grasped by his presence and his life. Our task as preachers is to help our congregations to be open to its witness, to be engaged by its testimony, and to be confronted by its kerygma. We present it, not as facts about Jesus as he was in Palestine, but as an inspired response to the Lord's risen and exalted presence in our midst. That there are facts there to be found is not to be denied. But to go grasping at them and to try to find our security and our life in them rather than in the present is not on. To try to do so must be to earn the rebuke delivered to Mary Magdalene at the tomb. To us as well as to her, the risen Jesus says, 'Do not hold me; for I have not yet ascended to the Father.' The disciples' attention, their commitment, their faith, and their response must be directed, not to a Jesus who walks on earth and who is just the continuing life of the one who walked in Palestine, comforting though that would be. The disciple must not constrain the risen Lord for to do so is to imperil the Lord's ascension – to stop him, in fact, from becoming truly the disciple's Lord. It is to make him less than he can be, to miss his real significance. It tries to find salvation in something less than he is, and so to find no salvation at all. Seeking to find him thus, leads only to his loss. It is the ascended, eternal, glorified but hidden Lord alone who saves.

And, if we let it run free, John's gospel has the supreme merit of allowing Christ to become our contemporary and so our Living Lord. I write this soon after returning from having taken a funeral at our local crematorium. Like many of us, I am grateful to the modern liturgiologists for making available a service which (provided it is used selectively and with that individuality which comes so naturally to the Anglican parson!) can speak meaningfully to twentieth-century mourners. Yet I always jib at its rendering of John 11.25–26. It is literally correct as a rendering of John's text. But it lacks the grandeur, the strength, and the contemporaneity of the Prayer Book version. Poetry has gone, and imagination has died. But, more important, a crude literalism has taken over and one which is itself shaped by a concern to see John's gospel primarily as a report of the past. A cerebral straightjacket has been forced upon what should be setting the tone of all that is to follow in the service. What comes over is arid and flat, witness to a concern with the past rather than with a proclamation for the present. There is no doubt that the Prayer Book version has caught the actual spirit of the Fourth Gospel which the modern translation sadly misses. It is the risen Lord who is the resurrection and the life as he confronts the disciple as his contemporary and as he meets him in an existential confrontation to bring hope, life, and rebirth. The discourses disclose what can be his significance for us, and the narratives portray this meaning in dramatic form. Through both, Jesus can become our contemporary – and so our Lord – and it is our task through our preaching of the Fourth Gospel to help and enable this to be so.

We do this in the pulpit through our overall attitude to the Fourth Gospel. We do not treat its witness as directed to the past but to the present. This does not mean, of course, that from the pulpit we discuss what did or what did not, what could or what could not have happened. We let our attitude come across through our overall approach, through the questions we ask of the text, through our general handling of John's work. We speak, for instance, of 'what John is trying to say through his telling of the story of Lazarus'. In our exposition of the text we say things like 'John has Jesus stay two days', 'John presents the raising of Lazarus as leading directly to a summoning of the Council which determines upon the death of Jesus.' All the time we turn the attention of our congregation to look for the insights that John is giving through his handling of his material. The message, the kerygma, becomes the point at which we encourage them to rest their gaze. And it is the same in the discourses. In our going through the text, we shall say things like 'John represents Jesus as saying', 'John has Jesus say', 'The Johannine Christ says', 'In John, Jesus is made to call himself the Vine'. We shall not be afraid to point to the differences between John and the synoptic gospels, and we shall say clearly that, overall in the Fourth Gospel, it is not easy to determine what Jesus actually said or to reconstruct the actual facts upon which the individual incidents are based. But, nevertheless, this is done, not in any negative manner, but through the way we draw out the meaning of the text that is before us. It rests, not upon particular discussions (though we will not avoid those when we are called upon to enter into them), but upon an overall approach, a gradual encouraging of an attitude, upon the validity of our insights, upon the worth of what we uncover and the effectiveness with which we are able to commend it.

We shall let John stand apart and we shall seek to commend the greatness of his achievement. This is not to 'dodge' the historical question but is to treat it in its wider context and to accept that – in John – the actual historical question is not the most important or even necessarily high upon our priorities. It is to commend John as what we believe him to be; it is to encourage others to look at him in this way; it is to ask of him questions to which answers of inestimable value can be given. The worth of the approach, the value of its insights, will encourage our congregations to accept John in this way. It will be found to satisfy as it becomes the means of enabling the risen Lord to confront us more effectively. Though in hard fact John's gospel throws up the question of history in its most acute form, in actual practice from the pulpit it does not do so. Its truth – the validity of its insights – its existential power takes over to give both fulfilment and satisfaction as it links up with our experience and causes that to be deepened and enriched. It is a question of our showing our enthusiasm for John and of carrying over something of our own conviction and expectations to our congregation.

The Fourth Gospel has always made a very strong appeal both to the English scholar and to the English churchman, and it has been as inspiring in its devotional use as it has been blessed by a remarkable succession of outstanding commentators upon its thought. Nevertheless, it has to be remembered that it remains one interpretation of the significance of Jesus, one that expresses a response which, though its undoubted inspiration is shown by its own continuing ability to inspire, remains nevertheless a response of a particular segment of the early Christian community. And it behoves us – indeed, our understanding of the gospels as a whole compels us – to ask whether John has got his response quite right. For we need to remember that, in the second century, John's gospel was almost taken over by the Gnostics. The earliest known commentary on John was written by a Gnostic. Orthodox Christianity was highly suspicious of John's work in the light of the use of it by the Gnostics who found that it could with little difficulty be accepted as an expression of their own outlook and could be used as a basis for the further extension of their ideas. It was not until the determined and authoritative advocacy of Irenaeus (who was bishop of Lyons at the end of the second century) that the Fourth Gospel was rescued from Gnostic clutches and restored to favour in the great church. Irenaeus was the first as far as we know to attribute it to the apostle John.

John's work was not popular in the early church and the early Fathers provide little evidence of its use. And the reason is exactly that which caused it to be greatly admired by the Gnostics – John so emphasizes the divinity of Jesus that there is a real danger of its overwhelming and submerging his humanity. There can be little doubt that John has in fact failed to take seriously the real humanity of Jesus which is so obvious in the synoptic presentation of him. This has a further result. John's attitude to 'the world' is highly ambiguous. God loves the world, yet Jesus is unable to pray for the world. Though the world is made by God, its real nature is such that it is unable to recognize its maker's presence and activity. The world therefore as 'world' is inevitably alien and opposed to God.

For all our admiration for John then and in spite of all that we learn from him – in spite of the fact that his work is a supreme means of our being united to the risen Christ as Lord – we have to acknowledge that the Fourth Gospel has real dangers for us.[7] It can obscure Jesus of Nazareth – it can cause us to lose him in the divine Lord – and can cause us to belittle the world for which Christ died. It can easily be open to misinterpretation: it can be taken over by false enthusiasms. That the danger is a real one is proved by the way this happened in the early years of its life, and it seems most likely that I John had to be written to counteract this danger. John's was an attempt to interpret Christ to a group of people whose background, beliefs, and intellectual climate were quite different from those of the synoptic writers. It was an inspired attempt to make Christianity intelligible to people of a different outlook from that of the mainstream of early believers. In doing this, it showed the way for all future efforts at communication. It set the seal of approval upon attempts to meet such needs, and it gave a magnificent exhibition of how the challenge should be faced. But it also revealed the dangers inherent in the enterprise. Interpretation can mean disturbing the balance of the original: it can result in a loss of something of the fact in the desire to express its significance.

Our interpretation of John – our use of it and our preaching through it – needs to be aware of these dangers. We need constantly to be treating it alongside both the synoptic gospels and the Old Testament, and to allow these to anchor both it and us when we are in danger of floating out into the deep waters of speculation, or when we are in danger of becoming so mesmerized by its greatness that we fail to treat it as one response amongst others, which together make up the total witness of the New Testament to Christ.

4

A Question of History

Our discussion of the Fourth Gospel has raised in an acute form the problem of the gospels and history. Indeed, for most people it is *the* problem presented by modern critical views for it seems to stab right at the heart of Christian truth, of Christian conviction, and of Christian assurance. If the gospels are not – at least in places – describing hard facts, if they seem to be 'writing up' what actually happened, then not only their credibility but ours also seems badly threatened. We may preach the gospels as testimony, as the evangelists' witness to Jesus – and we have suggested that this is in fact the way they must be preached – but this will bring to the fore the realization, not only that it seems to call in question some of the facts behind the faith, but also that it inevitably puts a question mark against the reliability of their testimony. The aim of this chapter therefore is to discuss the nature of the problem, to try to understand how we can approach it and to help our congregations to accept it, and to consider, nevertheless, how we can still trust the gospels and accept their witness with confidence.

It must be admitted at once that the gospel critics do not always appear to recognize the true nature of the problem that their work presents to the parish priest. There is a tendency among many of them to bypass the problem altogether either by denying that it exists or by ignoring it. The result is that their attitude is made to appear somewhat cavalier. Here, it seems to the general practitioner, the scholar is in danger of being esoteric and of playing word-games which have little to say to the man in the pew as he struggles to work out his faith against the realities of that indifference, not infrequently merging into contempt, which he sees around him. It is on this point that the scholar can legitimately be charged, not with disturbing faith by his conclusions – for there is nothing at all to be gained by concealing what is believed to be the truth in a cotton-wool which obscures what Christian belief really is – but with a certain insensitivity to those who are unable to share in his mental exercises or to have that knowledge which the total picture makes available to him.[1]

To those who look in upon the academic debate from outside there does appear to be something akin to perversity on the part of those scholars who easily deny the importance of events in the life of Jesus and who appear to deprecate facts as a question of legitimate concern on the part of those who place their faith in him. All too often it appears as though the message is elevated to a position where the facts are declared expendable. Questions about the historicity of the events in the life of Jesus will perplex for they seem to strike not only at the reasons for believing in Jesus but also at the integrity of the faith which the church proclaims in its creeds and in its worship. Moreover, if events are described as history which on inspection turn out to be not of the stuff of real history at all, then the actual beliefs of the evangelists become suspect too. It is right that we should ask the question 'Why should we believe in Jesus?' and it is not enough simply to answer 'Because others have done so'. Anyone with a television set is painfully aware that enthusiasm of belief is no guarantee of the truth of that which is believed. Fanaticism has its successes and wishful thinking is not necessarily transitory. It seems to us that we must be able to give a reason for the faith that is in us, and that means that we cannot ignore the question 'What really happened?' even if we cannot always answer it.

The critics' approach raises problems also about both the competence and validity of the evangelists' proclamations. We expect our historians to give us interpretations to which we can assent precisely because they are based upon facts that are true. We now write an adequate history of the Battle of Britain because we can, from a more distant perspective, come to a legitimate understanding of its significance, both for its contemporaries and for the later course of the war, and indeed we can see it contributing to a nation's understanding of its past. We would however expect the historian to try first to discover the facts – history as it really was. Wouldn't it be essential for instance to know exactly (or at least as exactly as we can) how many British and how many German planes were involved and shot down? I write this after watching one of A. J. P. Taylor's television lectures on 'How wars began'. On the origins of the First World War he made the point that new theories were required because only recently new diaries had been made available which gave new details thereby throwing new light upon both contemporary and later events. New facts had made possible a new and better

interpretation. Twentieth-century historians, no less than their somewhat despised nineteenth-century predecessors, honour facts as alone
providing a basis for legitimate interpretation. 'What actually happened?' is not a question of dubious intregity: it is a necessary basis for
response.[2]

Common sense suggests that the parish priest is right when he maintains that the critical approach to the gospels presents him with a very
real problem here. If it is by-passed, faith is liable to be confused with
wishful-thinking and a dialogue with the unbeliever becomes a virtual
impossibility. The difficulties must be faced, and the legitimacy of the
worries have to be acknowledged.

The extent of those worries were brought home to me recently when
I was leading some Bible study sessions on the Acts of the Apostles. I
had prepared some notes on the Pentecostal bestowal of the Spirit as it
is found in Acts 2 and was trying to show what Luke was striving to get
across to his readers through the way he told his story – of the significance as he saw it of the event as a whole and of its various parts – of
the tongues of fire, of the universal Jewish gathering, of the different
responses. I was pointing to Luke the proclaimer, to Luke the preacher.
And one of the group expressed a concern that was worrying her very
much indeed. Approaching it in this way suggested to her that doubt
was being cast upon the reliability of the actual report. I suggested that
this was not necessarily so, that the events were not necessarily brought
into question, that I was not setting out to make a value judgment upon
the facts that were reported to have happened. I was simply saying that
it was coming to us through Luke's eyes, that he was reporting it from
his point of view, that his description was a subjective one in that it was
made from the point of view of faith, that it was a verbal picture rather
than a photograph in words, that it was a witness to a faith as well as to
an event. But of course there was no denying that, once it was seen as
this, then the objectivity of the report, its actual literal accuracy as a
factual statement of what happened was inevitably called into question.
A question mark has to be set against events even if a negative answer
is by no means necessarily required. And the question mark itself is
enough to disturb. The tongues of fire might have been imagery, and
the speaking with tongues might not have meant a complete command
of all the necessary foreign languages.

Dealing with the events in the life of Jesus in this way is even more
disturbing. At an earlier meeting, we had been studying the Acts
account of the Ascension of Jesus and had inevitably compared it with

the ending of Luke's gospel. We also had to face the fact that Matthew
does not describe an Ascension though his last narrative barely leaves a
place for any later appearance, and that John implies an Ascension,
though it is not described and though it certainly does not bring the
resurrection appearances to an end. Again, I concentrated on the significance that Luke saw in the event – in the cloud, in the going up, in the
men's appearance, in the wistful gazing of the disciples – and also
pointed out how his whole gospel moved forward towards this climax.
This time, the problem of history was even more to the fore than it was
to be in the Pentecost session for now the differences between the gospels
made it acute. The more one talked in this way the more it seemed to
be the case that Luke's interpretative instincts were blurring his reporting concerns. At the end of the session, the parish priest expostulated
loudly that he wanted to make it clear that Luke's event could have
happened as he described it, and that my approach did not necessarily
mean that it did not. And, of course, this is true. Nevertheless, what was
happening was that the more we looked into things – the more we
appreciated what significance Luke saw in the details he recorded, and
the more we compared his approach with that found in the other gospels
– then the more we had to ask questions and as a consequence it was
unavoidable that we should leave a question mark over the actual historicity of the report. This approach is disturbing in so far as it means
that we cannot with certainty say where the evangelists' interpretative
skill begins and ends, and are therefore left with doubts over what
actually happened behind the event as they describe it. The parish
priest's interjection at the end of the session was an attempt to cushion
the uncertainty and to throw the balance of possibilities in favour of
historicity. It was the pastor's concern to reduce the perplexity and
doubt caused by the inevitable uncertainty.

Pastoral concerns – pastoral obligations and pastoral responsibilities
– will put great pressure upon the parish priest to come down on the
side of historicity. It will cause him to maximize the factual and to play
down the subjective act of interpretation.[3] Nevertheless, he would still
do well to be careful here. Pastoral effectiveness as a test of truth must
be handled with extreme caution. It no doubt encouraged the Jewish
leaders to continue in their rejection of the Christian proclamation of
the cross of Christ and, by itself, would not have caused Paul's contemporaries to accept the validity of his belief that the 'weakness of God
is stronger than men, and the foolishness of God is wiser than men'.
Though pastoral effectiveness must be brought to bear upon the work

of the critics, the results of that work must also be allowed to test our
evaluation of what pastoral effectiveness really is.

Our test of what is pastorally effective must in the end be, not what is
convenient but what is true and, even the test of what seems to work
and our evaluation of the needs of those to whom we minister, must in
the end give place to what the gospels reveal about themselves and of
what God really was doing in Christ.

And on this question of the gospels and history, we in the parishes
must face the fact that the critics are actually pointing to a real problem.
It is not raised merely by presuppositions which are themselves caused
by scepticism amounting to surrender to the spirit of the age. The
spirit of the age, it is true, encourages enquiry, rigorous sifting of the
evidence, a critical approach to the miraculous, and an appreciation of
the many-sided nature of the quest for truth. It is certainly other than
that of earlier ages and reveals itself in an undoubted questioning of
authority. But no one can doubt that these things have led to great
benefits to the world at large and that they are a part and parcel of mankind's legitimate development. It is therefore inevitable that the same
spirit of enquiry should be directed towards the gospels, and belief in
providence suggests that this is wholly right. The gospels are not to be
set apart from that concern for truth which is one of God's gifts to men.
We therefore have to be open to the questions that the critics are raising
and we have to avoid the temptation to rush too quickly to put up
defences which can in fact all too easily shut us off from their legitimate
insights. We are not compelled to accept their answers, but we are at
least required to follow the reasonings upon which they are based and
to deal adequately with the evidence they produce.

Perhaps the real nature of the difficulty can be tested by following
them in their study of the resurrection narratives, for these raise the
problem in an acute form and in a particularly sensitive area.[4] It is faith
in the resurrection of Jesus which lies at the very heart of the New
Testament proclamation and without this our preaching as well as theirs
would be vain. Of the strength of that faith there can be no doubt, but,
about the actual historical events which underlie it and which brought
it into being, there is room for much more uncertainty. However, it is
not just scepticism which causes such a judgment to be made, but a
recognition of the very real problems inherent in the biblical narratives
themselves when they are pressed to reveal strict historical facts.

When we compare the narratives of the four evangelists we see that
their accounts differ considerably. It is not merely a question of

differences in details though these are not insignificant. So there are
variations in the names and numbers of the women who went to the
tomb and also in their motives for going. More important, what (or
rather whom) they encounter there is described very differently. In
Mark they see a young man: in Matthew they behold an angel of the
Lord descending from heaven whose 'appearance was like lightning and
his raiment white as snow'. In Luke they encounter two men 'in dazzling
apparel': in John Mary Magdalene, who goes first to the tomb, and the
disciples who run there, see no one at all in the tomb and it is only later
that Mary beholds 'two angels in white, sitting where the body of Jesus
had lain'.

Even these differences, however, though small in themselves, are
not without significance. Differences, even contradictions, might be
expected in accounts of what must have been a confused and confusing
situation. However, such confusion is not enough by itself to account
for those differences in the gospel records for, so far from being circum-
stantial and the outcome of chance incorporation into the various narratives, they show rather the result of careful editing to make them fit
neatly and compactly into the overall outlook of the total narrative of
the gospel of which they are a part. What we have are not details differing as a result of varied traditions which are themselves caused by
confusion, but four consistent, highly organized, compactly argued and
clearly developed accounts by four evangelists where the theological
interpretation of each determines how particular events are described.
The distinctive outlook of the gospel writers determined what they
included and how they described it.

A more important discrepancy occurs in the location of the resurrection appearances. Mark, through the young man's message, implies that
they are to take place in Galilee. Matthew has a brief appearance to the
women near the tomb, but the real manifestation of Jesus takes place in
Galilee where he appears in his glorified state. Luke, on the other hand,
has a deliberate alteration of the message from the tomb which cuts out
any suggestion of Galilean appearances. In keeping with this he describes appearances only in the vicinity of Jerusalem, and the risen
Christ charges the 'eleven and those with them' not to depart from the
city until after the gift of the Spirit. Appearances in Galilee, which had
earlier been by-passed, seem now to be deliberately excluded by this
command. John 20 contains only appearances in Jerusalem, and the
original version of the gospel seems to have allowed for none in Galilee.
However it does not exclude them deliberately and in the gospel's

appendix in chapter 21 there is recorded a later appearance by Jesus there.

What are we to make of these differences? They are certainly of such a kind as to make it impossible to bring the four narratives together to display a single chronological order of events without doing considerable violence to at least one of the gospel accounts. Luke's record is the problem here and it is not possible to make room in his narrative for the appearances in Galilee without a hypothetical break in his record and one which is entirely without justification in the gospel itself.[5]

Luke's alterations show that he at least was sitting loose to history and that his account is theologically rather than historically determined. If he knew of appearances in Galilee, he chose to ignore them because they did not fit his scheme. For him they could only have been wayward events having little or no real significance. History was nothing unless it revealed theological truths: bare facts as such were of no importance. John again originally was not concerned with Galilee. The recognition of the true worth of Jesus had to take place in Jerusalem, for it was there that the true revelation of his glory had been made. But for Matthew, the significance of the resurrection was found rather in the universal witness to the glorification of Jesus. It was Galilee, the springboard of the new, rather than Jerusalem, the home – almost the tomb – of the old, which mattered. And for Mark – well, for him resurrection appearances as such had little significance. The future was all-important.

This means that their desire to give careful historical accuracy at this point seems not to have been very strong. The hard fact is that the gospel stories here do not enable an answer to be made to what are to us entirely legitimate questions, and that we must acknowledge this situation and rest, if not content, at least accepting in our ignorance. Otherwise, we try to turn the narratives into something which they are not and, in the attempt to answer our historical problems, open up for ourselves new problems which then become overwhelming.

One such – perhaps the most important of all if one tries to take the stories as though they were reporting hard history – is the nature of the Lord's risen appearances. It is not a question of the empty tomb, for all the evangelists witness to that, but their confusing descriptions of the Lord's resurrection state. In Matthew, Jesus appears as already glorified: Mark's expectation of the future revelation of Christ in glory is brought into the present. In John 20 Jesus, who seems already to have ascended to the Father, bestows the Spirit upon the disciples. The final action in the work of salvation is already accomplished. In Luke on the other hand, Jesus is not glorified until the Ascension. Only then can the disciples worship him and have that joy which comes from his exaltation. Until this further act, Jesus is in what has been called a sort of half-way house, risen but not yet advanced to his final position of authority. The Spirit could not be given until after this final act. His words to his followers await a future realization.

Once again this suggests that the evangelists are describing events in terms of their significance as they understood it rather than that they are trying to give literal descriptions of hard facts. This would also account for the seeming inconsistencies in the individual narratives, more particularly as these are given by Luke and John. Luke has Jesus walk with two disciples to Emmaus, but he remains wholly unrecognized until he takes part in the act of breaking the bread when he vanishes from their sight. Yet, in the very next story, he appears among the disciples, is recognized, has a real physical body which he demonstrates by eating before them, and then parts from them, not in some immediate vanishing act, but in a movement away from them. In John 20, Mary does not recognize him until he speaks. It is not his physical presence which really manifests him. Later, however, he shows his hands and his side to the disciples to confirm his resurrection, though when Thomas later demands proof, there is no need for Jesus' offer to be taken up. Nothing is said then about his leaving them. John 21 has a rather hide and seek attitude to the physical witness of Jesus to himself. The disciples know and yet do not know him from his appearance. Again, the importantance lies in the words and the actions.

To press the details here is to invite perplexity for oneself and incomprehension on the part of one's hearers. For, as literal statements, they will not fit and result only in a jigsaw puzzle where the individual pieces do not really come together. Certainly the evangelists did not mean them to be contained within straight edges for they merge directly into the present, to the Christians' contemporary experiences. In the light of the present, they describe a past event-experience, but do so in such a way that the past can be one with the present by providing its basis and perspective. They seek to answer the questions of the present with a certainty about the past – that is of the reality of the resurrection of Jesus and of his appearances to the early disciples – but they do so with their eyes set upon the questions of the present generation of disciples, and the appearances are described so as to have real bearing upon them. Past beginnings, present realities, and present questionings together produce the stories in the form that we now have them, and it is impossible to unravel their various parts. To understand them without each one of these parts is to do despite to the evangelists and disservice to our contemporaries.

The problems of history in the resurrection stories, then, are very real ones and arise directly out of the nature of the narratives themselves. They have to be faced therefore as much by the man in the parish as by the scholar for here is something which does not go unnoticed by many of those among whom we have to work out our witness. For the point is that doubts about exactly what the evangelists were up to when they composed their narratives, and what they were trying to convey through their material, are brought in, not by some extraneous reasoning, but by the nature of the material itself, by the differences in the several gospels, by the way those differences reflect and express different outlooks, and by the evangelists' seeming different attitude to history that these suggest from what we would expect. It is when the narratives are approached with the minimum of presuppositions – when we try to let them speak for themselves – that the problems about their attitude to history come to the fore. The narratives themselves suggest that we must face these problems and try to come to a right assessment of their significance. Our integrity – the truth of our witness to the living Lord – demands nothing less than this.

What then do the gospels suggest about the attitude of their authors to history? What does the way in which the evangelists seem to have gone about their work tell us about their approach to the events they recounted and through which they expressed their faith?

Our first point must be that the evangelists seem to have been more interested in giving us the significance of the event as they saw it rather than in presenting an account of just what happened. Differences in the evangelists' reporting of the same event – for instance, the trial of Jesus before the high priest – make this judgment inevitable.[6] More than that, they conveyed the significance in the form of actual reporting so that, in part at any rate, the significance of what they saw in any episode determined what they wrote. Facts were in some way subordinate to significance or, if that seems too strong, they were at least capable of being hostages to significance and to the meaning which the evangelists wished to convey to their readers.

But we cannot stop there. All the evangelists' differences cannot be accounted for on the assumption that they were just drawing out or clarifying what was already there. Their writing up was not simply in the nature of a paraphrase. At times quite deliberate alterations seem to have been made to what was before them. Take for instance the request of the Sons of Zebedee for a position of authority in Jesus' kingdom as this is found in Mark 10 and Matthew 20.[7] In Mark the request is made by the disciples themselves: in Matthew Jesus is approached by the disciples' mother and the form of the request is less demanding, less harsh, less presumptious. How did Matthew arrive at the form of his story? Did he alter Mark or did he have another source to which he gave preference? Whatever the nature of his sources, Matthew's narrative can hardly have been arrived at on the basis of objective considerations for, since Mark's is the more 'difficult' version of the incident and therefore more open to alteration, it is almost certainly nearer to the original factors. But Matthew's conclusions were determined by something other than impartial investigation. Matthew knew his risen Lord, he experienced his risen presence, and he therefore knew how his disciples, now reverenced by Matthew's church, would have acted. For him therefore, it 'must' have been the mother. Nothing else was appropriate to the present belief and to Matthew's sense of oneness with the past. He had a further source of legitimate information about the past: it was his own sense of openness to the indwelling spirit of Christ his contemporary.

The evangelists wrote about Jesus, not as a figure of the past, but of the present. The resurrection meant that he now lived in them as they lived only through him. They had found life in him, and he was known to them through his living, active presence in the Christian community of which they were a part. Therefore alongside their written sources, alongside the traditions of Jesus that were handed down in the community and which had themselves been shaped by the community, they had another source for their knowledge of the past. It was the living Jesus in their midst, and his experienced presence could shape, refine, clarify, and correct what other sources contained. They had a sense of oneness with Jesus which not only told them what he was now, but also determined their understanding of what he was and must have been then.

This understanding of the present as a valid source of information about the past was made the more real to the evangelists by their position as the successors of that line of recorders of God's action which is contained in the Old Testament. The evangelists were men of the book – they were inheritors of the outlook of Israel as that was shaped by its possession of the Old Testament. And history for the Old Testament was never an objective account of past events. It was a recital of God's glorious deeds on behalf of Israel, and what these were, how they were told, was determined as much by what the present revealed about them as by an investigation into past history. For the present revealed either the climax or the nature of those deeds. History was not a closed book. The present gave an invaluable clue, not merely to the significance of past events, but also to what those events really were – to what happened and to what caused the significance they saw in the events. And so the Old Testament gave a picture of past events as they were seen through the eyes of faith as the Jews year by year expressed their oneness with the past through their cultic participation in the event. That it caused those events to be 'written up' there is no doubt.[8]

Our evangelists were heirs to this outlook. It must have entered deeply into their thinking and was, of course, made even more prominent by their sense of Jesus' living presence in them now.

But their possession of the Old Testament affected the evangelists' handling of the story of Jesus in a further way. In their hands, the Old Testament became a means of justifying their faith in Jesus. Jewish rejection of him was countered by the claim that he fulfilled Old Testament expectations and so could be accepted as the Messiah who had been promised of old. In a very early statement of belief, Paul writes that 'Christ died for our sins according to the scriptures' (I Cor. 15.3), and Luke says that on the way to Emmaus, the risen Jesus 'beginning from Moses and all the prophets interpreted to them in all the scriptures the things concerning himself' (Luke 24.27). The scriptures as a whole were seen as pointing forward to Jesus. They were therefore searched for texts to justify the events of his time on earth. More than that, however, because he was seen both as the fulfilment of Old Testament expectations and also as the culmination of God's saving activity as it was revealed in the Old Testament, the Old Testament itself became a source of information about him. What the Old Testament said about the coming saviour must have happened in Jesus, and how the Old Testament described the earlier part of God's saving deed must have found fulfilment in the final part. Consequently its descriptions of the coming leader, its hopes for the future, and the manner in which it described God's earlier redemptive acts could all be used as sources of information about the life of Jesus. The Old Testament spoke about him. And so it told Christians about his life and ministry.

The Old Testament therefore exerted a truly creative influence upon the traditions of Jesus that were handed down in the church and upon the evangelists themselves as they set out – more deliberately and calculatingly – to write their gospels. In the first place, it would cause them to write up events. An example of this is found in Matthew's account of Jesus' triumphal entry into Jerusalem. Using Mark as a source, he expands it by introducing an explicit quotation from Zechariah 9.9 which, though underlying Mark's episode, is not actually quoted by him. He allows this to determine his expansion and more especially he introduces both an ass and a colt because a parallelism seems to require them. Mark's episode described a less explicit claim on the part of Jesus and limited the recognition of him to the disciples who enthused about the coming kingdom rather than about Jesus himself. Matthew on the other hand not only makes Jesus' claim crystal clear, he allows it to be recognized by crowds of people and to result in the climax, 'And when he entered Jerusalem, all the city was stirred, saying, "Who is this?" And the crowds said, "This is Jesus of Nazareth of Galilee." '

But it is very possible that what was done by Matthew had already been begun by Mark and his predecessors. It is strange that the incident resulted in no reprisals from the Roman authorities. Whatever Jewish feelings were, it is unlikely that the Romans could have afforded to ignore the episode or that Pilate's unwillingness to condemn Jesus could have followed such a scene. In the light of their beliefs and of their use of scripture, the evangelists almost certainly enhance something which was originally more enigmatic and less open. The evangelists are filling the event with the significance it had for them.[9]

Above all, the Old Testament was searched for information about the Passion of Jesus both to justify his rejection by the Jews and his death upon a cross, and also to give information about his attitude to it. Their accounts of the Passion are written around an amalgam of Old Testament quotations, allusions, and prefigurations. That these illustrations have a role which is greater than that of mere illuminations of events which happened to Jesus is made almost certain by the fact that different evangelists show the influence of different Old Testament prefigurations. Their different presentations of Jesus – for instance their different words from the cross – are caused not just by their glimpsing different sides of an elusive figure, but by their being influenced by different Old Testament ideas.[10]

The Old Testament had a truly creative influence. It seems to be causing the evangelists, not merely to slant their descriptions, but actually to create a number of the events themselves. It not only influenced the way they described events in Jesus' life, it seems also to have determined what some of those events actually were. It is never easy to say exactly where this is happening, but the important point is that this possibility has always to be allowed for. So, for instance, it was probably the Old Testament expectations of what would happen at the Last Days which caused Luke to limit Jesus' resurrection appearances to Jerusalem and its environs, to think of Jesus' Ascension in the way he does, and to shape his description of Pentecost as he has. One can never be sure, but the possibility has to be allowed for, and his differences from the other evangelists and his consistency in presentation together turn the possibility into a strong probability. Throughout the gospels, the Old Testament exerts a truly creative role as it was accepted as an inspired, divine witness to Jesus the Christ.

If their use of the Old Testament marks out the evangelists as being very different from us, the thing which pinpoints the difference most clearly is certainly their attitude to history and to historical reporting. This caused them to use the historical method as a means of proclaiming their beliefs which, in their descriptions of any event, seem to have been their primary concern. History was in some way an open book. Their beliefs controlled their reporting of it; their theology often determined what it contained. So, Luke's Ascension narrative is there because it is the ideal vehicle of his theology and it is just not possible to say what 'hard' history it embraces. All that can be concluded is that Luke would not have felt our dilemma. His Ascension story is controlled by his understanding of the whole career of Jesus. It points back to the beginnings of that story and, indeed, beyond it to the whole history of God's saving acts in Israel. Matthew, likewise, ends his gospel with a narrative which encapsulates and develops what his gospel as a whole has proclaimed as 'God with us'. Now, at the end of his life, Jesus promises his enduring presence in the church. The end points back to the beginning and affirms its proclamation. What really happened at Jesus' final meeting with the disciples seems beyond recovery. The evangelists do not set out to make that clear. What they aim to do is to share their convictions, to proclaim their faith, to express their certainties – and they do this through the medium of historical writing. Their writings are a response to Jesus crucified, risen, and worshipped.

All this can help us to understand the evangelists and their attitude to history. It can describe their approach and can help us to appreciate it. However, it does raise a dilemma for us for it shows us that the criteria the evangelists used to determine what they wrote and how they described it are other than what we would expect them to have been, and are in fact other than the ones we would use for determining the validity of their portrait of Jesus. For the evangelists proclaim not merely a faith in Jesus, they are not merely their testimonies to him; the gospels purport to give reasons also for accepting the validity of those testimonies. The evangelists were not only proclaiming Jesus, they were giving reasons which would enable their readers to acknowledge the rightness of that proclamation. Those reasons, however, do not have the same validity for us since we do not share their evaluation of the Old Testament's significance and we do not see history as an open book. We live in an age of hard facts, and we are unable either to deny their significance or to allow faith to stand as a substitute for them.

We are therefore compelled to wonder whether we can still trust the gospels. The gap between the evangelists' attitude to history and our own makes this imperative. For many, it still seems that the gospels must either be taken as 'real' history, that is as true accounts of what actually happened during the life of Jesus, or else be dismissed and all faith in them be lost. Many, both within our congregations and among the more sceptical and critical of our contemporaries, would see the gospels in this way – either as 'true' or 'not true', their truth or falsehood being determined by how accurately they reported the facts of the life of Jesus. Does our new realization of what the evangelists were doing, and our new understanding of how they approached their tasks, mean that we can still use them to deepen our faith, or are their credibility and our faith both dangerously undermined?

We should, of course, be clear what we mean by these questions. If by 'trusting' the gospels we mean using them to arrive at a number of solid, clear facts which can give us absolute certainty about God's action in Jesus and an incontestible criterion for expressing our faith in him, then the answer must be a firm 'no'. The gospels do not allow us certainty about what happened in the life-time of Jesus; they cannot give us 'hard' factual evidence for the rightness of our beliefs. And it is important to remember that, rightly understood, they have never done so. The evangelists' contemporaries could have accepted them as facts – they would have had no difficulty in doing that – but the facts themselves could not have made them believe. There was not really anything in the life of Jesus which gave unambiguous proof of what the evangelists claimed, and such witness to him as was made by various incidents in his life was annulled by his crucifixion which upended all expectations and seemingly reversed any possible 'proofs' that could be brought forward. All the evangelists were conscious of the need for faith and were well aware that any belief that sought an open vindication for the life of Jesus was an empty shell. The cross would not allow for that then, and it is equally certain that it cannot allow it now.

Nevertheless, Christianity is no flight from reason, and it does assert that God has acted in history in the life, death, and resurrection of Jesus, and that that action is itself the paradigm as well as the focus of all God's action in the world. Indifference to what actually happened in that life seems to be both a denial of God's action in the world and a flight into irrationality. Most of us therefore – and one suspects most of those to whom we preach and who have to live out their faith in relationship with those around them – would want to feel that the gospels make a fair assessment of Jesus and provide a fair response to him which, though made against the background of beliefs of their day, can still be used by us. We need to feel that their response to Jesus is a legitimate one and that we can still go through it to recover a Jesus who was of such a kind as to make both their response reasonable and our response a rational one, even though its rightness can neither be proved nor be openly verified.

To be able to give a positive answer to our question 'Can we trust the gospels?' therefore we need to be able to assert two things: that we can still use their story to arrive at some picture of Jesus as he was, and that the person discovered is such as to suggest that the evangelists' portrait of him and their proclamation about him together make a legitimate response to him – only though remembering that both their picture and their response are shaped by their preliminary beliefs which spring from their age and their tradition. In this way we can then go on to make our own response which is one of true faith and not of irrationality.

Can the gospels pass this test? Can we continue to have confidence in them? Two things suggest that we can.[11] In the first place, there is a striking difference between our gospels and those which we call apochryphal which is of such a kind as to suggest that they have an authenticity which others lack. They have not tried to hide the ambiguity of Jesus and they have not resolved the essential dilemma which Jesus presented to those who believed in him. John has nearly done so, but his approach seems only to bring out the constraints under which the synoptists were writing. Secondly, such a belief as they express, which is at once both overwhelmingly powerful to them but also not without formidable difficulties for them, is not easily explained as self-generated. On the contrary, such a difficult belief, such an unobvious faith, would seem to require some special significant happening to have caused it to have come into being. These two arguments are ultimately of the nature

of value-judgments upon the gospels and, indeed, upon the validity of
the early Christian community and, further, of its present manifestation.
Nothing of a more objective kind is possible but the life of Jesus itself
suggests that nothing of a more objective nature should be sought. God
acted only in hiddenness, and the ambiguity of the cross suggests that a
search for more open, unassailable demonstrations of him is both futile
and actually wrong.

The gospels can in fact enable us to see through their witness a Jesus
of history who was of such a kind as to set their response in motion.
Through their reporting in faith, we can have a glimpse of one whose
life, death, and resurrection brought their response into being and who
can summon us both to learn from their response and to share in its
commitment. For their response is rooted in history and is still controlled by that history. Here their status as inheritors of Israel's attitude
to historical reporting is important. Whilst it caused them to interpret
history and made it 'open' to them in a way that we would not find
acceptable now, it nevertheless rooted them in history and stopped them
from going off into uncontrolled speculation. They did not forget nor
deny the problem of Jesus' history. John, actually comes closer to doing
that and he needs the synoptics and the Old Testament to anchor him.
But the first three gospels never did. They were faithful to the ambiguities of Jesus' earthly life and they were aware that these can be faced and
overcome (not, indeed, denied or avoided) only in the light of the
resurrection. It is only when – as on the road to Emmaus – it is viewed
in the light of the resurrection that the Old Testament can really point
to the validity of the cross. Before then, its witness is both hidden and
not easily apprehended. When the earthly Jesus justifies his suffering
by reference to the Old Testament, he meets only incomprehension.
The Old Testament itself needs his resurrection to enable its witness to
be clearly understood. That the evangelists did not resolve the problem
of Jesus' history, and that they linked him firmly to the Old Testament
is of the greatest significance in enabling us to accept their basic truth.

If all this suggests that the evangelists' witness can be accepted as
having a firm root in true history which has not gone off into the realm
of wild, uncontrolled, speculation, then the magnitude of the response
which they present can itself also witness to the power of what set it all
in motion. Not only is the response rooted in an historical event, the
enthusiasm of the response itself witnesses to the greatness of that
event. The response of the gospels, and the kerygmatic picture which
enshrines that response, are both real parts of the history of Jesus for

together they unpack the impetus which was part and parcel of his whole event. The response witnesses to the reality of the life of Jesus and to the dynamic that was found in it. The kerygmatic picture is a vital part of the whole action and is an integral act in what, in the jargon of today, comes together to make up the total 'Jesus event'.

It witnesses in the first place of course to the impact of the resurrection and to the continuing apprehension of Jesus through the evangelists' share in the new community of faith. But the resurrection did not occur in a vacuum. The risen Jesus was known only because his earthly life anticipated and began a relationship that could be cemented and deepened as it was welcomed and embraced. The risen presence in the community could be received as joyful and life-giving only because some in his life-time had already experienced the beginnings of that freedom brought about by him. His resurrection could be understood as part and parcel of God's final redemptive, eschatological act only because the kingdom of God had already been experienced in his person.

The resurrection presence needed the life, and the response is witness in truth to the validity of that life. Stories of Jesus' life could not therefore be made up in a vacuum or become unrelated to their beginnings. The nature of the Christian experience was such as to demand some form of answer to the question of 'how it all began', and 'how we got to where we are'. History was problemmatical for the early church, and this meant that the history of Jesus could be neither totally transformed nor wholly ignored.

We can then continue to have confidence in the gospels. Modern critical study has not undermined this but has given us valuable insights into the nature of their witness to Jesus which enables us to use their response to deepen, sustain, and inform our own. Modern study has, it is true, called into question many of the assumptions that have been made about the gospels and their relation to the history of Jesus, but it has at the same time allowed us to be more honest about the difficulties in the older assumptions, to be more aware of the true nature of the gospel records, and to come to terms with the problems they present. It has allowed us to have a more open approach to them which, though it does of course owe much to the spirit of the age, is nevertheless a part of that quest for truth which is the work of the moving Spirit of God in our midst. That that quest can sometimes take wrong turnings should be a cause of humility in our approach rather than a reason for denying its validity. As the Johannine Christ says of the Spirit's work, 'He will take of mine and declare it unto you.' I believe that this new appreciation of the evangelists' attitude to history is a part of his continuing work of doing just that.[12]

Yet there is no denying the problems that this new attitude causes those who are parish priests for it appears to call into question things which we once took as certainties, things like the virgin birth, the empty tomb, the miracles, and so on, for it questions whether the gospels themselves provide hard and fast statements of facts which can form the basis on which these beliefs can rest. It denies certainty for it suggests that the gospels can no longer be taken for granted as presentations of objective reports, as actual descriptions of clearly defined events. They have to be sifted for facts, and when they are so sifted, they cannot always give us certain evidence of what happened in the life of Jesus. And it is this which causes distress and instinctively draws us into a defence of the old ways and into an attack upon modern criticism.

This is wholly understandable for, not only is our commitment at stake and our whole stance threatened, but what we know deep down to be true, what is part of our deepest conviction – that upon which we are formed and by which we know ourselves alone to live – is called into question. Modern criticism seems not only to challenge the nature of our commitment – that of itself is not necessarily a bad thing for the nature of our response, its validity, must always be questioned in the light of our deeper entry into the things of Christ. More vital, however, it appears to be denying that by which we live and have our being. And this is far more serious for it seems to be demanding of us that denial which was demanded of the early martyrs, the refusal of which led them to the stake. It appears in truth to be asking us to deny ourselves, and this we cannot do. It is this which instinctively makes us draw up our defences for it appears to be denying that faith to which we are committed and which is expressed and found in the Christian community which maintains us and unites us to the Christ in whom we believe. We are asked, we think, to deny not only ourselves but also the community wherein we have found Christ and encountered his reality. We think that we are being asked to turn our backs upon something we have found to be very precious and which we know to be part of the truth of our existence.

Such a response, however, is by no means required, and it rests upon a misunderstanding of the significance of what modern criticism has to say about the gospels and history. What modern criticism has done is not necessarily to deny the truth of those events to which the biblical narratives bear witness but rather to suggest that those narratives cannot of themselves form the basis from which the truth of the events can be determined. What we have in the biblical narratives are not objective accounts which provide records of the beginnings of the church's tradition, nor are they photographs which can give us records of the events in a by-passing of that tradition. What we have are descriptions formed in the light of the tradition of the church, not guarantees of the truth of that tradition. So, for instance, belief in the virgin birth of Jesus rests, not upon either Matthew's or Luke's accounts which cannot really be harmonized and which cannot of themselves bear the weight of rigorous historical enquiry, but upon the tradition to which they bear witness and from which they spring. The validity of the tradition will be judged rather by its own strength, its conformity to the whole life of Jesus, its continuing ability to inform, its appropriateness to Christian truth, and the inner assent both of the community and its individual member.[13]

The New Testament witnesses to the early church's faith in Jesus; it gives expression to the beliefs of the early Christian community and describes the events of Jesus' life in terms of those beliefs. It invites us not to find in it literal descriptions of some hard and fast events which brought that belief into being, but to share in its response and so to believe in him whose earthly life as well as his resurrection was of such a kind as to set it all in motion. It cannot, of itself, give us concrete, objective reports and it cannot therefore give us some kind of hard and fast reason for believing in its events. It can offer no more than a freezing of the church's tradition through the work of a particular evangelist at a particular time and in a particular place. It gives us no source of information, no extra guarantee, other than, and as a part of, the faith of the church. It is a summons to us to join in that faith rather than an independent guarantee of the rightness of that belief.[14]

This then is how we preach the gospels and their witness to the events of Jesus. It will of course mean that the facts of Jesus' life will be seen as less certain than we once thought, and we will have to allow that this makes for greater variety of beliefs among modern Christians. We will have to let our congregations see that recent understanding of the gospels makes this inevitable and we shall help them to see that an absolute conformity of belief has never at any time been established by the church at large. The New Testament itself witnesses to a variety of ways in which response to the work of God in Christ was expressed.[15]

This openness cannot give that certainty which some may want, but there is nothing at all to suggest that, whenever Christianity has been understood properly, it has provided such a thing. When John penned the ending of his gospel and wrote: 'Now Jesus did many other signs in the presence of the disciples which are not written in this book, but these are written that you may believe that Jesus is the Christ, the Son of God, and that believing you may have life in his name,' he was maintaining that Christians could walk only by faith and not by sight. Luke's handling of Mark shows that the 'truth' he wanted to present to Theophilus could be guaranteed only by faith rather than by strict historical accuracy. In the same way, we present the gospels as powerful statements of faith in which we can be brought to share by the fervour and the validity of their writers' witness. We shall help our congregations to enter into them with sympathy and with imagination. The result will be less clear-cut than in the past we have perhaps expected it to be, but it will nevertheless be real and perhaps more in keeping with the outlook of the evangelists themselves.

5

A Word for Us

Modern criticism of the gospels has encouraged us to see them as part and parcel of the response of the early church to the life, death, and resurrection of Jesus. They were written as the evangelists' testimony to what they knew had happened in their midst and their aim was to encourage others to share in their witness and to have their own response deepened and enriched thereby. In our earlier chapters, I suggested therefore that this is how we should preach them to our congregations. This approach, however, raised the question of the gospels and history. In the last chapter, I asserted that the problem, though real, was not insurmountable. The gospels were based on a real history to which they could be accepted as legitimate responses in the light of the whole event of Jesus.

However, though this understanding enables us to continue to have trust in the gospels and their testimony, it does, nevertheless, underline the fact that the outlook of the gospel writers was very different from our own. They had a very different approach to the significance of the Old Testament as a creative force in informing the Christian response to Jesus and they used a very different approach to facts. What constituted a legitimate basis for determining facts and for describing events was quite other for them than it has to be for us. Moreover, what they did describe, they expressed in accordance with the religious, intellectual, and cultural understandings of the day. Their place as men of the first century determined how the events were understood by them and therefore in what terms they were to be recounted to their readers.

There is then a very real gap between their outlook and ours. They were men of the first century and we are men and women of the twentieth. They were writing to their contemporaries who could share in their outlook and their understanding. We are very different at both these points and the modern approach to the gospels seems to bring this out very clearly. Their proclamation may have been very appropriate and very compelling in their day. The question which must concern us, though, is this: Can their proclamation do anything for us in our day? Can it address us with anything like the same clarity and the same conviction as that with which it addressed the early church? Can its message impinge upon members of our congregation now?

Put baldly like that, the question may sound absurd, and perhaps it is. But that should not hide from us the fact, as we saw in our first chapter, that the Bible is very widely disregarded in the church at large and by individual members of our congregations. Yet, we set out to try to restore it to its proper place, and we seem only to have succeeded in revealing its distance from us and its strangeness to us. For the hard fact is that modern critical study, by restoring the gospels to their rightful place in the first century, has at the same time, in the first instance at any rate, distanced them from us.

A few years ago, I completed a study of Luke's writings which brought home to me the real nature of the problem which modern criticism has put before us.[1] After making that study, I felt that as a preacher I was in a position to enable my congregation to understand what Luke the preacher, the pastoral theologian, was about when he wrote his gospel and then followed it up by composing the Acts of the Apostles. I felt that I had been able to establish a certain empathy with his writings and that I could therefore help my listeners to enter imaginatively into them and so to appreciate the gospel he was proclaiming.

Nevertheless, I was also very conscious that, in one sense at any rate, my new understanding also made the task of preaching more difficult. It wasn't just the fact that Luke's attitude to history and historical reporting was different from ours, though, as we have seen, this is complicated enough and was going to present real problems of emphasis and approach, and indeed of outlook, every time I mounted the pulpit. But I had long been aware of these and was convinced enough in my own mind about both the importance of the problem and the necessity of facing it to make the tackling of it worthwhile. I believed that a right approach to it would deepen a congregation's understanding of Christianity, would enhance their appreciation of the Bible, would help to remove unnecessary stumbling-blocks, and that it would also help to build bridges between them and the world at large. In other words, I was convinced of the potential value of this approach, and believed that our concerns both for the congregation and for truth at this point led decidedly in the same direction.

My new problem, though not unrelated to the question of the evangelists' attitude to history, was in fact wider than that. If I was right in my understanding of Luke, then the questions he was tackling when he wrote his two volumes were very much questions of his own day rather than of ours and, since the answers that he gave were also expressed in terms of his own times, the points at which they made contact with our questions and so helped to frame our answers were inevitably very much reduced. The questions Luke faced were centred largely upon two things, namely, the failure of the Parousia to happen, and the failure of the Jews to acknowledge Jesus. These highlighted one more problem which was the seeming absurdity of the Christian claim that the cross, and indeed the life of which it was the climax, was in fact God's answer to the needs of the world.

Now, obviously Luke's questions are not completely unrelated to some of our own day. Like him and his readers, we are concerned about the hiddenness of the Christ – about the lack of his open sovereignty over the world – and we are troubled by the apparent inability of our times to see relevance in Jesus and by the general failure of our generation to respond to him. But our questions do not find their focal point either in the Parousia or in the attitude of the Jews. We do not continue to long for the return of Christ and so for us the present, seen as the product of a long-continuing history must stand, as it were, on its own feet. Again, we cannot find our answer to its problems by viewing our history as the fulfilment of the Old Testament record of God's promises. We cannot use these to seek legitimacy in the events of our own times. Nor, yet again, is the life of Jesus given some guarantee for us by its conformity to the Old Testament pattern and ideal. Luke's faith in the Old Testament, though illuminating, can move us little, and his concern with the expectations of the people of Israel can interest us even less. We no longer see them as our people, and we are not interested in seeing our history in relation to that of the Old Testament. We do not look upon Abraham and his kind as our ancestors and we are much more conscious of the break which Jesus made with the past, with the element of discontinuity that was inevitably and rightly introduced through him. We can respect the Old Testament and learn much from it, but it is too much to ask our congregations to take its history as their own.

Because our questions, though related to Luke's, are genuinely other than his, his answers, fashioned by expectations of a Parousia and guaranteed for him by beliefs about the truth of the Old Testament, can have little direct significance for us. This is the problem for the preacher.

Does Luke, as Luke, have anything meaningful to say to us? Can his answers to problems of his day help us to find answers to very different problems of ours? Can his proclamation of Jesus as Christ and Lord help us to be found by God through him today? Can his beliefs deepen our response and make us more open to the God who has to be discovered in the very different world of the twentieth century? In a word, does recognizing Luke's distance – his otherness – from us mean that we have to leave him in his own, other world, or can we pass over, be informed, and then return, enriched and deepened into our own?

In trying to rescue the Bible from indifference have we then just gone round full circle, and are we left virtually encouraging our congregations to leave it in its mothballs? The severity of this reaction to our approach to the gospels must cause us to pause and to ask whether there is not an easier entry – and perhaps therefore a more legitimate one – into their message than that which we have been advocating. Does the difficulty itself in fact witness to a built-in illegitimacy in our approach? Are we pursuing a wrong method and ignoring a more direct way of making our congregations open to the evangelists' work? We cannot, it is true, go back to the more conservative approach to the gospels which accepts them primarily as an accurate historical witness to Jesus as he was on earth. Such an approach could only ignore the true insights of modern criticism and result in effect in what we believe to be a misunderstanding of the evangelists' testimony. But is there another way which, though acknowledging the fact that the evangelists' attitude to history differs from ours, can nevertheless bypass this to allow the gospels to have a more immediate address to us? Can we virtually ignore what any passage meant to the evangelist and his contemporaries and concentrate instead on what it can mean for us? Would it not actually be better to let our imagination run free to encounter the Bible as it is, to let it open up insights and ideas by our just, as it were, sitting under it and seeing what it can then do for us?

After all, many of our fellow-preachers do not allow themselves to become bogged-down by questions about the original events and the original meaning of those events in the minds of the evangelists. They find, rather, a meaning in them now. The gospels speak to them, and through them to their congregations, of surrender, of freedom, of new life in Christ, of a real apprehension by God through him. These are the things that matter, and if they are not more immediately the outcome of the gospels as they are understood in the light of their original meaning, that really is beside the point. They come to the Bible with expectancy, and the reality of its inspiration is seen in its continuing ability to inspire. So in the hands of such preachers, Jesus' Transfiguration becomes primarily a pointer to our own through him, his resurrection a means of expressing our new life in him, his Ascension the point at which we find our entry into the heavenly places with him, and so on. The miracles witness to the miracle of grace in our own lives, to our wholeness through Christ, and to our rebirth in the life of the Spirit. They become signs in the Johannine mould of the nature of God's remaking of us through the whole work of Christ.

Such an approach to the gospels can prove to be both powerful and compelling, and through it they can become lively expositions of grace, of challenge, and of appeal. Certainly, it makes for relevance and seems to impinge directly upon the congregation. It is in effect an existential understanding and proclamation. It leaves aside questions of the original meaning – both of the event itself and of its significance for the evangelists and their contemporaries – and approaches the gospels with an expectancy which finds a significant address in them for our contemporaries and which makes for a response which embraces not merely the head but also the heart and will. We bring to bear upon any passage of the gospels our imagination, our insights and our understanding as these have been informed by the wisdom of the ages and, when in fact we are prepared to do this, the text is found to address us in a way which is both new and newly-releasing.

Such an approach would mean accepting the evangelists primarily as tellers of stories which contained insights and possibilities that are far greater than they themselves realized when they wrote them. Once these stories were written, they encapsulated a power of their own which was capable of envigorating the whole personality of each of those who accepted them; they became the vehicles of God's direct address which opened the reader or listener to his grace and life. Accepted by the church and fashioned into a canon, they then assumed a givenness which was further deepened and enriched through their use down the ages which brought to them an added dimension and treasury of insight. This deepens their power to impinge upon us every time we 'break the word' and sit under its judgment.

This outlook comes close to some of the insights of those who advocate what is known as the 'New Hermeneutic' which insists that the meaning of any passage of the gospels is to be found in the passage ✓ itself. It cannot be separated out or extracted from it to enable it to be expressed completely in any other way. The text is a well which runs deep.[2]

Nevertheless, even exponents of this method insist that we do not turn our backs on biblical criticism but maintain that in order to be really effective it must build upon the valid insights of the critics and their work. The real impact of the biblical text can only be felt when its utter strangeness – its true distance from us – is allowed. Only so can a real dialogue with the texts be entered upon and only in this way can their power to shatter and recreate become truly liberated. However, in practice this critical approach is seemingly restricted to the preliminary investigations of the text, for it would appear to fall away when the interpreter dons the mantle of the literary critic or comes to the text with an expectancy of an address dictated by his own presuppositions. The text becomes proclamation – it becomes a 'word event' which stirs the whole man, is then itself illuminated by the whole man, who is himself in turn again grasped and moved by this new understanding. The possibilities are enormous and the power thus released can flow in all kinds of new directions.

In many ways this approach is both exciting and envigorating. Nevertheless, it cannot alone really deal with the whole of the gospels, and attempts to make it do so would seem to be dangerous. It issues in confidence by avoiding the difficulties and it avoids the difficulties ultimately by ignoring them. And the basic difficulty is that, as we have seen, the Christian proclamation, the fundamental kerygma of the gospels, indeed the gospel itself, is expressed, not merely in an address, but also in a statement. The claim of the gospels is not merely that they contain a declaration which is heard compellingly and releasingly as it is brought into speech, but also that they impart information which is the basis of their address and which alone enables the proclamation to be really of the nature of good news. The appeal depends upon a proclamation which itself and in its own terms cannot be divorced from an event. In the literary or existential approach, when this is carried out fully and with an enthusiasm displayed by its most able practitioners, the story aspect appears to have taken over completely. The 'truth' of the story seems to be found in its ability to appeal to its hearers and ultimately to move them rather than in its truth as a genuine response to that which it purports to contain and which needs to be seen as buried legitimately within it. In the last resort, it tends to bypass history and to find truth in something divorced from it. Ultimately, therefore, it tends to play down the essential challenge of the cross which consists in the historicality of the event itself and of the life which led up to it. It avoids the enigma, and so it misses the elusive quality of the character who hangs upon it.

No preaching which does not do justice to the fact that Christianity is based upon an event in history – and which does not wrestle with the significance of Christianity's relation to the event and to that event's witness to the God who stands over and beyond it, and yet who is revealed in and through it – no preaching which does not do that can ✓ really be said to convey the heart of the saving proclamation. Without that, the proclamation is very lacking and is, indeed, ultimately unreal. It is highly significant that one writer who is by no means unsympathetic to this line of approach has to admit that even in the parables, which by common consent have been most illuminated by this method, the application has led to banalities in the actual end-products. The promise of the method has not brought about an equivalent value in the results.[3]

Moreover, this approach has led to a preaching which is in real danger of becoming elitist in its attitude. It can engender an outlook which appears to be capable of being apprehended only by those who can 'see' things in a particular kind of way, who are prepared themselves to ignore the scandal of history and to approach the gospels wholly through imagery and symbols, to see their truth in a timeless series of insights made possible by this particular stance. It can at worst inculcate a kind of superiority born out of an attitude akin to Gnosticism rather than that humility and openness which should spring from faith. Even at its best, though it might open up some lines of communication with those who are unable to accept the more historical approach to the gospels, it would appear to do so only at the expense of genuine theological discourse.[4]

The fundamental weakness of this approach to the interpretation of the gospels is that, in fact, it divorces Christianity from history. Christianity is not a response to a book but to a person. This approach gives little thought to what really happened in the life of Jesus, ignores the fact that the gospels were written at a particular moment in time, and pays scant attention to the fact that we have to live out our faith in relation to the ambiguities provided by history around us. This means that there is something of a jump in its treatment of the gospels. It can either ignore the problem of what happened in the life of Jesus, by treating the gospels' descriptions as pure story having little more relation to fact than the contents of a parable, and then see what emotional, spiritual, and artistic appeal this makes to us now, or it can treat the event – for example a miracle – as one that actually happened in the life of Jesus and then go on to use that as an illustration of the spiritual and psychological wholeness that Jesus can bring us. Either way, however, shows little respect for the intellectual questions of modern men – the former by ignoring them, and the latter by engaging in some verbal ambiguities which try to conceal the fact that the term 'miracle' is being used in two totally different ways.

But the gospels are not indifferent to history, either to that of Jesus or to that of their contemporaries. They are concerned with history and therefore cannot be properly understood without reference to the history of Jesus himself and to the church situation which was the immediate cause of their production. Their witness is given at a particular time and place and in the light of a particular situation, and that is something we need to remember if ever we are to use them at a very different period in time and against the background of a very different situation.

Our first act in the process of interpretation, therefore, is to enter as sympathetically as we possibly can into their situation, into their outlook into their understanding. This is not easy.[5] It means coming to terms with the 'pastness of the past' and breaking into it and facing all the problems of different outlooks that are suggested by the term 'cultural relativism.'[6]

We have already seen this supremely in the evangelists' outlook on history and in their understanding of the authority of the Old Testament. Their approach here was so different from ours that it is almost impossible to understand that it was an entirely legitimate one for men of their day and of their presuppositions. But we have to do this if we are to make sense of the gospels. More than that though, we have to have such sympathy with their approach that we can then go on to learn from their proclamation even though it is given in a form of which we, as twentieth-century men and women, can no longer really approve. Anyone who has tried to explain the evangelists' outlook to a group of sceptical schoolchildren or even to a group of moderately sympathetic schoolteachers will know just how difficult it is to get them to come to terms with, much more so to appreciate, an outlook which is so other than their own.

However, the difficulties, which must be fully appreciated if we are to do any sort of justice to the task, should not deter us from setting out upon it. And when we try to accomplish this from the pulpit we are setting out from a position of very great advantage for we are linked to the evangelists and their writings by a common faith – not so much a common system of belief as a common experience, a common sharing in the community of those whose hearts have been touched and whose outlook has been transformed by a living Lord whose presence is found in worship which by its very nature incorporates us into that timeless response which has been the lot of the Christian community of every age. We are linked to the experience of early ages and it is this common response formed out of the interdependence of every generation which enables us to make a genuine contact with the cerebral which expresses the experience, and which gives the beliefs of earlier generations a chance of being understood by us.

It is this common experience of the saving grace of God through Christ that can enable us to appreciate the outlook of the evangelists and to have some empathy with their work even if it is shaped by presuppositions and expectations which are so very different from our own. It is true, of course, that however sensitive our interpretation, however sympathetic our outlook, we can never enter completely into their thinking. Because our world is not wholly open to invasion by hostile powers as was their world, because ours is not a plastic world to be moulded by God completely as his power directs, because it is not one that is to be destroyed at the precise moment God wills, we do not have the same sense of the instability of the moment. Our attitude to wonder, to dependance, even to obedience is inevitably different from theirs. Our knowledge makes both for different understanding and different expectations. There is a real sense in which man has come of age and we know that we stand on our own feet in a way that the ancient world just could not envisage. Their understanding of God must inevitably be very different from ours for their expectations and ours just do not coincide. We simply can never actually feel, think, understand, or even experience in the way that they did. Nevertheless, this does not mean that we should not be asked to try to understand how they felt. Imagination can enable us to enter into their situation – not of ourselves – but as they might have seen it. We are not asked to relive their situation, but we can legitimately be called upon to try to understand what it must have been like for them. The difference can be illustrated by a simple example. Some years ago, it was the policy of those responsible for the training of ordinands to encourage them to work in a factory for a year or two before going on to theological college. At one stage the requirement was raised almost to the status of a dogma, for it was felt that this would enable the ordinand to get inside the mind of the worker and to understand how he felt.

Quite apart from the inverted snobbery that was inherent in the exercise, it had a built-in weakness because it was based largely on pretence, on pretending that the ordinand was one with the factory hand whereas in fact his situation was totally different. Background, general outlook, and above all the knowledge that he was doing the job for only a limited period meant that he came nowhere near to the same position as the worker who was going to spend all his life doing the job. For the ordinand it resulted so often in a false situation and a false outlook. It was better to recognize the difference, to accept that identification was impossible, but to realize that this did not rule out understanding, respect, sympathy, and a deeper awareness of sharing in a common humanity.

It is the same if we try to be one with the biblical writers. In one sense we cannot. Our experience, our outlook, our expectations, our under-standing just do not coincide with theirs. But we can nevertheless try from our outside position to understand how it must have been for them. We cannot exactly 'think their thoughts after them' but we can try to imagine what they must have been thinking. We shall never get it exactly right, but we can at least have a real imaginative insight into how they felt. We have to feel our way into their work, and this means a long, difficult process. We cannot easily and quickly make a bridge between their world and ours. There are no short-cuts for, if we attempt to take them, we shall end up with something which, though it may seem immediately relevant, is usually rather superficial if not facile, and lacks the depth and the validity which a more legitimate appreciation of the significance of the gospels can bring.

The seriousness of the problem is easily illustrated. At the heart of Jesus' message was his proclamation of the coming of the kingdom of God. How are we to understand this? The Thanksgiving Prayer in the first revision of the Anglican Eucharist (Series Two) included in the anamnesis the phrase 'And we look for the coming of his Kingdom'. What did that mean in the minds of most Christians as they heard it at the heart of the eucharist? No doubt to most of them it suggested a community that was more open to the sway of Jesus in a world that was more responsive to him. It looked to a future for mankind where the will of God and the love of men was in evidence. Such possible thoughts, however, were obviously not acceptable to the liturgical revisers and in the next revision the phrase was altered to become 'And we look for his coming in glory'. The change could of course be defended on the grounds of liturgical accuracy since the other parts of the prayer are directed to actions within the career of Christ himself, but one suspects that the real reason for the change was brought about by that biblical conservatism that was so much a part of the revised service. We are to hope for what the New Testament hoped and our interpretative instincts are to be kept in control by biblical authority. But what expectations are contained in the biblical hope of the coming of the kingdom? It would come in its fullness, they believed, only at the Parousia when Christ would return to judge not only those who claimed to follow him, but also, and perhaps primarily, those who had rejected the Christian proclamation. Whilst Luke can see Christ's coming as the time of hope for his sorely tested followers: 'Now when these things begin to take place, look up and raise your heads, because your redemption is drawing near', he sees it also as a time of judgment upon the world at large: 'Remember Lot's wife. . . . There will be two women grinding together; one will be taken and the other left.' The gospels see little of positive hope for the world in the proclamation of the coming of the kingdom. For them it is rather the winding up of this present world order: it is 'tribulation such as there has not been the like from the beginning of creation which God created until now, and never shall be. And except the Lord had shortened the days, no flesh would have been saved. But for the elects' sake whom he chose, he shortened the days.'

The New Testament expectation of the return of Christ is conveyed through apocalyptic imagery. It is possible indeed to see the beginnings of a break-out from the constraints brought about by that imagery as the full experience of Jesus was allowed to break through its presuppositions. So we have a kind of two-stage eschatology where the kingdom, though primarily future, is seen in the light of Christ as being partially present. As this is realized more, so the judgment of the future upon the present and its cancelling out of the things that now are will have to be played down. But the New Testament has not yet come to this stage and the apocalyptic outlook which still controls its thought will not allow it to move forward with the freedom that the coming of Jesus demands.

This means that their view of the world is not a positive one. It is significant that Billy Graham in a recent television interview about a mission he conducted in communist Poland admitted that he had been very slow in coming to appreciate the social implications of the Christian gospel. An apocalyptic world-view based on a conservative acceptance of the gospels had in fact blinded him to this dimension of the gospel and means still that his moves towards embracing it are half-hearted and inevitably ill-defined. This view is not far removed from that outlook found in any sectarian gathering represented on many a beach on almost any day in summer where the proclamation is that the Lord is at hand, that he comes with glory to reward the elect and to wreak vengeance upon those who continue to deny him. Embarrassing though this may be for us, and however much we may try to dissociate ourselves from it by pulling our coat collars over our dog collars and by slipping unobtrusively away, it remains a fact that this proclamation stands much closer to that actually found in the gospels than is our message of hope, of renewal, and of world-acceptance. That it is also less Christian seems certain.

Such then is the real measure of our difficulty when we come to preach from the gospels. First, we must recognize the difficulty by giving full value to their otherness. Our problem can then be stated thus: Given that the Gospels are response to the whole work of God in Christ and that they were made at a particular time and against a particular background, and in the light of a particular 'world-view', how can these responses still inform our response to Christ? How can their otherness be used to deepen our proclamation?

The answer is to be found, I believe, in the way of dialogue. Our task in the pulpit – and indeed whenever we use the gospels – is to enter into dialogue with them, to learn from them as we accept them as supremely important responses to the whole work of God in Christ, to put questions to them which are framed in the light of our problems and of our apprehension of God's manner of working in the world as it is, and at the same time to put their proclamation and their answers under the critical scrutiny of a deeper understanding of the whole work of Christ which the contribution of some two thousand years of Christian witness and perception enables us to have.

Some years ago in the biblical set texts papers of the ordination examination there used to be a question demanding what was called an exposition. It caused a constant headache because just what an exposition entailed was open to a variety of interpretations. Overall, it came to be suggested that what was required was an unfolding of (a) what the passage meant then and (b) what it means to us now. Such a rubric seemed to suggest that we ought to be able to move straight from the original meaning to apply its significance directly into one of an equivalent nature for us now. So for example, when Ezekiel was the set text, a part of his vision could be expected to have some significant meaning for us now and one which was of equivalent significance to that which it had for his contemporaries. What was required was a process of translation, of updating.

This however is just not on. All parts of the Bible – event parts of the gospels themselves – cannot have a direct, compelling message to us now, and one which we must take as complete in itself, as an expression of a full response to God's work in Christ. The way of dialogue, however, does not suggest that they should. It rather uses the gospel passage as a tool for coming to a greater understanding of God's address which it finds in the present, not directly from the passage itself, but from the passage seen as a supremely important means in enabling an openness to Jesus our contemporary. The way of dialogue accepts the gospel narratives as supremely important responses to the work of God in Christ – and indeed as an actual part of that work – but says that our task is to use them not just through translation to arrive at an equivalent response on our part, but rather, through dialogue with them, to come to an appropriate response for us which takes into consideration, not only them, but also the continuing work of God's Spirit when he guides the church towards all truth as he takes the things of Jesus and draws them out to each new age.

We use them as supremely valuable witnesses whose testimony can make us open to the Word of God now as we learn not only from them, but also from the growing understanding of the meaning of Jesus, from the whole life of the church, from the world around us as it witnesses to the action of God in its midst, and from our own experience of the presence of the living Jesus in us now. The gospels become our primary witness, but they are a witness which has to be examined critically in the light of those other ways in which the Spirit of God works and by which the living Christ is known.

Our first task then (as we have seen) is to understand as clearly as we can what the gospels meant to their original readers as they received what was the evangelists' testimony to their contemporaries. A number of steps then follow by which it becomes possible for us to use them as a way – indeed as *the* way – by which God can address us now.

The first step in our dialogue is to acknowledge the individual witness of the different gospels and, by comparing and contrasting these, to allow them to throw light upon each other, sometimes by drawing out and deepening each other's understanding, and at other times by correcting it and revealing its limitations. If we are to use the gospels legitimately, we must both acknowledge and embrace the fact that each of them has its own particular understanding of what God has done through Jesus and therefore of how God was and is present in him. They represent individual responses – albeit ones formed out of the witness of a community – and they express distinctive theologies which cannot simply be harmonized and brought together without both distorting what they are saying individually and making of them other – and almost inevitably less – than they actually are. It is important that each gospel should be read on its own terms rather than through lenses provided by the contributions of the other evangelists. So, for instance, Mark's temptation narrative should not be read in terms of those of Matthew and Luke, and Matthew's account of the visit of the Wise Men should not be seen as having that element of hiddenness which is such an essential part of Luke's story. Harmonization inevitably leads to distortion.

More than that, however, there are places where there are not only differences, but also tensions. It is, for instance, not easy to fit Matthew's last scene with its understanding of a glorified Lord exercising his presence and his role in the church into Luke's ascension story which describes a moment of glorification which is also a departure to the heavenly sphere and an abiding there. The absent Lord now sends his Spirit upon the disciples. Or again, there are points of conflict between the theologies of Luke and John. It is difficult to bring together Luke's understanding of the Spirit-conception of Jesus with John's thought of the incarnation of a pre-existent Logos. The two ideas represent two different presentations of Jesus. The individual gospels represent a contribution to the developing understanding of Jesus rather than the whole of the Christian proclamation. We may want to judge their responses in the light of the creeds and to understand them in terms derived from these, but we should not read them as expressions of that kind of unified and developed theology which the creeds actually affirm.

Many years ago, now, the late Professor Hodgson in his Gifford Lectures aptly titled *For Faith and Freedom* stated: 'As one who has been a professional teacher of theology for forty-three years, I now publicly declare my hope that no pupil of mine will ever be guilty of using the expression, "The Bible says . . .".'[7] He was thinking primarily of that habit of supporting a belief with a biblical text which was then taken as justifying total biblical approval for what was being put forward. Most of us would not want to do this, and its illegitimacy has often been pointed out – though, alas, it is surprising how widespread the habit still is – but Professor Hodgson's strictures should be extended to include that form of argument which seeks to find a single outlook in the New Testament and to declare that *this* is legitimate for all time. Invariably, such a practice – which actually begins with a belief which it then seeks to justify from the Bible – fails to do justice to the variety of outlooks which the gospels exhibit and to the fact that no particular position in them therefore can claim finality.

The second step in the way of dialogue is one that acknowledges that the forms of the evangelists' proclamations are inevitably determined by the outlook of their day and more especially by that world-view which they had in common with their contemporaries. The evangelists were men of their times and their descriptions were controlled by the beliefs of those times. They expressed their own beliefs in forms determined by the first-century world outlook and in a way comprehensible to their readers. The content of their testimony to us, therefore, is not simply to be identified with the form in which it is expressed.

Most of us give what is at least lip-service to this point. Few of us would accept Paul's ruling about women and hats still less the reason behind it – or feel constrained by his assertions about the superiority of the unmarried state. We would accept that the gospels think in terms of a three-tier universe, of a god 'up there', and that their authors tended to visualize God as a man writ large. We would accept evolution and would recognize the folly of a church when it persecuted a Galileo and condemned a Darwin. We would allow that both episodes arose out of a misunderstanding of the real nature of the biblical revelation. Few of us would take the biblical accounts of the Devil's encounter with Jesus at his temptation as literal descriptions. Most of us have at some time or other deplored the hymn 'There's a friend for little children above the bright blue sky' and so we would not read Luke's description of the Ascension as a completely factual account of an actual event. We would hesitate to suggest that the heavens were literally opened at the baptism of Jesus or that there was a real, audible voice either then or at the Transfiguration.

Yet we fail often to see the real significance of the position we adopt. Where is the line between form and content to be drawn? At what point do we say that the writers are going beyond accidental expressions – determined by the world-outlook which they happened to have because of their involvement as real people in the prevailing culture of their times – to maintain that they are declaring something which is an essential part of the truth about God's dealings with the world in Jesus? The problem is to know when one passes from the inessential to the necessary, from the secondary thought-form to the genuine truth of revelation. Most readers of the gospels accept that they contain both elements. Differences arise over the points at which it is declared that transient form ends and essential content begins.

It is now generally recognized for instance that the creation narratives are to be accepted as myths, as pre-scientific statements about the creation of the world and of man and that their value for us lies in their attitude to life rather than in any facts that they claim to give. The oft-used saying that, whereas science states the 'how' of creation, religious statements express the 'why behind the how' is not without its merits. Yet the Bible itself views the creation narratives as more than this. It rehearses them as a series of events, and the creation of the world itself is given the status of the first in a series of historical happenings which is at the same time presented as the first of God's saving acts. The fact is that, whereas the Bible itself accepts these narratives as statements of factual happenings, as descriptions of actual events which were really thought to have taken place in the historical process, we have to accept them rather as refinements of myths which express insights into the nature of God, of his relation to the world and to mankind. But if we do this for statements about the world's beginnings, it seems very reasonable, if not essential, that we should approach its descriptions of the world's end in the same way. The gospels' descriptions of the Parousia, even their expectations of it, are no less mythological than the Old Testament's accounts of creation. They express the same world-outlook, and actually describe the end in terms of its beginning. We should then see both as expressions of value-judgments, of beliefs, rather than as descriptions of what actually occurs in history at its beginning and its end.

In an oft-quoted sentence, Rudolf Bultmann wrote: 'It is impossible to use electric light and the wireless and to avail ourselves of modern medical and surgical discoveries and at the same time to believe in the New Testament world of demons and spirits.'[8] This is of course an exaggeration – witness the fact that many people are able to believe precisely that – which both gives undue value to the god termed 'modern thought' and also gravely underestimates the credulity of modern man. Modern discoveries have actually made impossible far fewer of the biblical beliefs than this position suggests. Nevertheless, the important thing for us at the moment is the realization that belief in angels and demons is not necessarily demanded by their presence in the pages of the gospels. They may be seen as part of the form of the gospels' proclamation and as determined by the world-outlook of the first century rather than as an essential part of the Christian expression of God's work through Jesus.

Here, however, we are meeting that further difficulty presented by the fact that form and content cannot always be clearly separated; it is not always easy to distinguish between them and so to decide whether what is expressed is merely a part of the outlook of the age or whether it contains something which transcends that to express some truth of revelation. Belief in angels is a case in point. They may be just a part of the common outlook of the first century AD and, as such, may be seen merely to proclaim a belief in the care and in the immediacy of God's concern for, and address to, his people. As such, belief in them, though it is accepted as a good thing for men of those days, is accepted as unnecessary for us now since they are made virtually redundant by our understanding of God as Spirit and by our belief in the Trinity which expresses not only the holiness of God but also his abiding presence with us. We no longer believe in them, though we accept the beliefs that they were designed to express.

More than that, though, we might feel that to continue to believe in them is actually wrong for in themselves they would seem to witness to an outlook on God which full understanding of the significance of Jesus declares to be inadequate. The fact of Jesus means that all intermediaries between us and God are made, not only wholly unnecessary, but also illegitimate. On the other hand, again, we might feel that belief in angels expresses the truth that this creation does not exhaust the creative power of God and that the angels point to the full reality of the spiritual world. They can then express the conviction that the final reality within and beyond the world is personal rather than impersonal.

The result of our use of the gospels' belief in angels, then, will be different for different people. Some will see them purely as part of the early beliefs of man and will feel that our greater understanding must leave them behind. Some will see Christ as making them superfluous and will maintain that to continue to believe in them is actually detrimental to a true understanding of the nature and significance of God. Others will see them as pointing to a truth about reality which is valuable though they will not take the gospel belief in them literally. Yet others, however, will feel that their presence in the gospels witnesses to a literal belief in some other creation, to some other order of beings more open to the love and service of God than is mankind.

We are not offered a completely watertight guide as to where transitory form in the gospels ends and actual substance begins. All that can be said with confidence is that both are interwoven in the gospel records and that our handling of them must give due recognition to this fact.

This discussion, however, has pinpointed the fact that the evangelists' part in the general outlook of their day affected not merely their telling of the story but also the actual beliefs they expressed through the story. They expressed their accounts of the significance of Jesus – they imparted their theology – in terms of the general cultural, religious, and intellectual outlooks of the groups to which they were writing and of which they were a real part. These outlooks therefore determined the way they expressed their understanding of what God had done and was doing through Jesus, and how he was actually present in him. So, it is Luke's place in that line of thought which flowed from the historical and prophetic books of the Old Testament which made him describe God's presence in Jesus in the way that he does. Jesus is the supreme prophet, the agent of God, subordinate to God, exalted to the right hand of God. Luke's christology is essentially determined by his devotion to the Old Testament and this makes him present Jesus as the spirit-filled servant figure empowered and enthroned by God. John's place, on the other hand, in that twilight zone where Jewish, Greek, and Gnostic thought-forms met and interpenetrated each other determines his more ontological approach to the person of Jesus, to his pre-existence, his oneness with the Father, and to his indwelling of the disciples. Luke's background caused him to espouse a christology which was primarily functional whilst John's background led him into the realm of speculation about his actual nature. But both expressed their understanding in accordance with their backgrounds. Their previous beliefs determined how they described the fact of Jesus. And what is true of them is true of the earlier developments in christology. Jesus was presented to different groups in terms which drew upon the cultural and religious backgrounds of those groups. The great variety of christological positions in the New Testament is to be explained, not only by the growing appreciation of the full significance of Jesus – by that ongoing attempt to express the meaning of the impact he had made and was making upon them – but also by the necessity of commending him to groups of differing backgrounds and beliefs. Missionary preaching demanded that he should be proclaimed in different terms and through various images. The continuing life of the church meant that its embracing of these images affected in turn its estimate of him. That the structures of belief are secondary and not necessarily final is suggested by this very variety in the New Testament and by the fact that some of them were already in the process of being abandoned as newer structures were used. The structure of belief was always subservient to the reality. It remains a means rather than an end in itself.

The gospels, then, witness to the reality of Jesus in their own way. Their insights – their testimonies – are expressed in a way – in a form and through a structure – which is determined by an understanding of the world which is common to them and their readers. It is their witness rather than their actual way of expressing it which is of ultimate significance for us: it is their insights rather than the forms which necessarily contain these which must actually inform us. Sometimes the form will be deemed essential to the contents, but this judgment will be made only when the whole significance of Jesus seems to demand it. Equally however, restatement will seek to do full justice to the contents of their original proclamation of Jesus and will only depart from it if again the whole act of God seems to require it. The late Professor Hodgson was accustomed to maintain that the question we should ask of the biblical documents was one which had to be expressed in words something like 'What must the truth have been and be if it appeared like that to people who wrote and thought as they did?' Given their background, their general understanding of the world and of life, given their presuppositions, they described their response to, and their understanding of, what had happened in their midst in their own particular way. We have different presuppositions; our understanding both of the world and of people, our thought about God and his relation to the world is very different from theirs. How then are we to describe our response to an event which was of such a kind as to force such a response from them? We necessarily see both the event and the response to the event in a way very different from theirs. If something meant that for them, what was the reality of that something, and what should it mean for us?

Our third step in the process of entering into dialogue with the evangelists follows on from our discussion of angels and of the gospels' expectation of the kingdom. It suggests that our dialogue must embrace, not merely the form of their message, but its content also. It means not merely translating what they are saying, but sometimes actually refashioning it. The evangelists were men of their age, with the outlook, presuppositions, and background of their age. These inevitably put constraints upon them and stopped the full significance of Jesus from being seen. Jesus demanded a total reversal of old outlooks; his cross meant a complete upending of all previous expectations. It took time for the full impact of this to be appreciated; it took time for a true appreciation of Jesus to shatter and transform the expectations of those who had set out on the path of following him.

So, as we have seen, the evangelists tended to view him in terms of the apocalyptic beliefs of their day. They had not yet fully appreciated how these had to be stood on their head, how the coming of Jesus had passed a judgment on them, how their attitude to the world had to move on from rejection to acceptance, from denial to affirmation (albeit one tempered by a continuing tension with the world), from judgment to forgiveness.

Again, they hadn't yet come to terms with the fact that at the heart of the Christ-event was to be found a cross. Paul could say that the cross proclaimed 'My power is made perfect in your weakness' (II Cor. 12.9) and could accept that this made foolish all his boastings, but he could still engage in controversies with his opponents which exhibit no little rancour, personal spleen, and sometimes even downright bad temper. The cross had not yet completely become a way of life for him. At times he still seemed to be looking for some other vindication. It has been suggested that Paul's understanding of the resurrection of Jesus in terms of his vindication by the Father reflects a position which has not yet espoused the ultimate significance of the cross.[9] Whilst not all would agree with this particular point, it does nevertheless assert the fact that to be in keeping with the cross, any vindication of Jesus which the resurrection provided had to remain a hidden one, available only to the eyes of faith and not capable of any external unambiguous proof. The early church expected a final vindication to take place at the Parousia when Jesus' exaltation would be made openly visible for all to see. But the Parousia did not come, and a true appreciation of the significance of the cross and of the hiddenness of any vindication that was actually given through the resurrection suggests that the Parousia expectation was a result of a failure on the part of the early church to learn the real lessons that the event of Jesus should have taught them. Jesus was not going to be vindicated – they were not going to be vindicated – openly and unambiguously for all to see.

The fact that the gospels contain less than perfect responses to the whole event of Jesus means that our response is not necessarily to be controlled by theirs. Matthew's continued veneration of the Mosaic Law, Mark's focussing of everything upon the Parousia, Luke's impersonal understanding of the Spirit, John's playing down of the value of the earthly – these and many other limitations mean that our response, though informed supremely by theirs, though made in the light of theirs, though standing under the strict scrutiny and judgment of theirs, is not necessarily to be defined completely by them. Our attitude must inevitably be more universally directed, more appreciative of the wider workings of God in the world, more open to the strivings of the human spirit. Above all, it will be ever more aware of the insights into the significance of Jesus that nearly two thousand years of Christian history have provided. The idea of 'the faith once delivered to the saints' is not one that does justice either to the continuing activity of the Holy Spirit or to the God of the Bible who gives himself to men through a cross, or even again to the biblical understanding of itself.

Such, then, are the steps by which we believe it is possible to make a use of the gospels in our preaching which does justice to their true nature and which at the same time can use them both to deepen our own understanding of the whole work of God in Christ, and so also to make us more open to the living Lord. In summary, it means in the first place accepting the gospels as responses to the living Lord which have been worked out against the background of their age and in the light of the particular outlooks and problems of their individual churches. Since such an outlook was inevitably very different from our own, it demands a great deal of effort, of sympathy, and of imagination on our part. But all this is made worthwhile, for Christian experience has found them to be means of real encounter with Christ. We enter into a dialogue with them which involves accepting the various kerygmata of the evangelists. Secondly, it means taking into account the fact that the form of their proclamation is dictated by the outlook of the age and that this necessitates a considerable exercise in translation. The third requirement, however, was to go beyond the process of translation, and actually to examine the message of the evangelists in the light of some two thousand years of Christian witness and of the continuing enlightenment of the Spirit of God. We are under the judgment of the evangelists, but this judgment is seen to be limited by its place in time so that it is itself enlarged and corrected by the continuing understanding of the Christian community as it has responded to the presence of the living Lord in its midst and as it has been continually regrasped and extended by its response to Jesus of Nazareth.

But are we doing justice to the traditional belief in the inspiration of the Bible, a belief which, so far from being an academic and doctrinal imposition, gives genuine expression to the actual experience of countless generations of Christians. As Professor Bicknell expressed it, 'The Bible is supremely inspired because it has been found to be supremely inspiring.' Are we, on the other hand, letting modern assertiveness and confidence in its own judgments have undue influence upon our thinking? Are we, indeed, forgetting those countless thousands who today still find that the Bible confronts them with an authority that establishes it as the Word of God for them?

Again, we have to go back to the Bible and try to understand its inspiration in its own terms. Unless we are to hold some view which maintains that 'What the Bible says, God says', we must accept that it is actually in the writers themselves rather than in the actual words they use where inspiration is ultimately to be sought. Any doctrine of inspiration which seeks its subject in the text rather than in the authors of the text forgets that God through the incarnation spoke through a person rather than in a thing, that a static form of inspiration was an importation of late Judaism into Christianity and one which Jesus and Paul, by their attitudes to the law, declared totally inadequate, and that the text of the Bible itself was not so sacred as to prevent later hands from adapting, revising, and amending it. The Old Testament prophets witness to the fact that inspiration does not mean a total overriding of the human personality. Scholars have tried to describe their inspiration as concentration rather than absorption, as an indwelling of the Word rather than of the ecstatic Spirit. Their contemporaries were given no external guarantees by which they could distinguish them from the false prophets. It was simply that they were 'in tune' with God, whilst others were not. But that fact did not stop Jeremiah from uttering imprecations upon his enemies or Isaiah from having a total confidence in the enduring sanctity of Jerusalem which had to be denied by Jeremiah and which time itself ultimately proved to be false.

In the New Testament itself, Peter could fall into error even after the resurrection. As Paul so bitterly declared, 'And the rest of the Jews dissembled likewise with him: insomuch that even Barnabas was carried away with their dissimulation' (Gal. 2.13). Some of Paul's outbursts reflect his own personality rather than a total inspiration. Many of his positions have limitations which are inevitable in arguments that are addressed *ad homines*. His assertion, 'I have become all things to all men, that I may by all means save some' (I Cor. 9.22) means that they should not be taken out of their context but that they are often shaped by the exigencies of the situation. His thought undoubtedly developed over the years.

Again, the fact that there are four gospels inevitably implies limitations of the part of the individual ones. When Matthew and Luke took over Mark, it was not just a question of adding more parts, but was one also of revising, altering, adding and subtracting, and reshaping. Luke's prologue seems inevitably to point to some limitations on the part of his predecessors in the field, and these certainly included Mark and, probably, Matthew too. John when he composed his gospel, seems to have intended to counteract what were in his eyes the deficiencies of the synoptics, most likely by supplementing them, thought the possibility of his meaning to replace them cannot be ruled out.

The Bible itself suggests that inspiration does not mean an acceptance of the perfection of what is put before us, neither does it suggest that the tradition that is there crystallized is thereby meant to be fossilized. The tradition has been frozen at a certain point. For that we can be grateful since it represents a singularly splendid encapsulation of Jewish and Christian thought, but that this is the final, unalterable authority, the definitive statement, that this is to be identified with and made into the unhindered embodiment of the Word of God himself is ruled out by the Bible's witness to itself.

Above all, it has been ruled out by the fact of Jesus and by the response to him in the Christian assertion of the incarnation which maintains that God is found through a real human being. Because of that, it means that God is found also, even though less fully, in the human reasonings of other human beings as they respond to him who is the focal point of the revelation. Jesus means that God speaks through real human beings and not through cyphers. Only in Jesus himself was the perfect response made which enabled him to be called '*The* Word of God'.

That God can and does speak through the Bible is beyond doubt. That it must be accorded a vital, if not supreme, place in enabling God to encounter us is made certain by its impact through the ages. But it is secondary and derivative, having its inspiration not in itself but in its ability to let God be real to us, in its power to inform our response to Christ, in its value as a word of God enabling us to be open to The Word of God.

The way of dialogue offers a way of interpreting the gospels that does justice to the original witness of the evangelists, to the continuing history of Christianity, and to those valid insights which the ongoing Spirit of God makes available to us today. We have these books. They are our earliest witness to Jesus and to the faith of the earliest church. They remain our fullest and most authoritative source from which to build up our picture of Jesus, imperfect though we know that picture must be.

They have been a source of inspiration throughout the history of the church and at times have been the means of recalling it to its true nature and of setting it out once more on something like its right way. At times, they have nevertheless, led both to distortions and excesses, though even these have usually restored something of what had fallen into decay by reason of neglect or denial. Often they have been misunderstood, frequently they have been resisted. But through it all they have exercised an enduring power, a continuing fascination, an irresistible compulsion, a magnetism, a dynamic which has impelled the scholar to uncover their hidden depths in order to discover ever more clearly the one to whom they point, has opened new insights to the preacher, and has, above all, made the Christ, and through him the God who stands behind him, a reality for countless multitudes. This may not make for what can grandly be called a doctrine of inspiration, it does not give them an authority which puts them outside the reach of other authorities or which separates them off from the works of other men. But it recognizes that they are the works of visionaries who were in touch with God, and it acknowledges that even now they can help to make us more open to his continuing presence.

The aim of our study, of our preaching, and of our prayer is that Jesus should genuinely become Christ for us and for those to whom we minister: that he should meet us, confront us, judge us, and renew us. As he becomes Christ for us, so he becomes God's Word to us, making God real to us and uniting us to him. Through him we are found by God and so are united to the ground of our being and to the source of our life. That is our aim and it is at the same time our deepest need. The gospels themselves play the crucial part in bringing this about. We approach their proclamation with a sense of expectancy, for they enshrine the responses of the Christian community at the truly creative period of its history. They capture the early enthusiasm, the imagination that has been newly-released by the discovery of the significance of Jesus. They still speak to us with a vitality and power which comes from their being true instruments of the risen Lord. We go to them to be found by him, and we return from them more truly linked to him. To use them is to discover their value, to be deepened by their faith, to be enriched by their inspiration. In other words, it is to be grasped more effectively by God.

6

Preaching Jesus

The story often used to be told of the famous preacher who placed before himself in the pulpit the text, 'Sir, we would see Jesus'. It was there to remind him of the object of his preaching and of the nature of its contents. It said, simply and inescapably, that the task of the preacher was nothing less than to reveal Jesus – to make him more available to the congregation for their freedom and their life. Salvation was in him alone. On the face of it, the message was clear – or was it? Just what is entailed in 'seeing Jesus'? What picture of him are we to put before our congregations? More than that, in what dimension, from what vantage point, are we to present him? What did John, for instance, think that he was doing when he wrote his gospel to put Jesus before his readers? Did he think that he was showing them the Jesus who stood before the Greeks when they made their request to Philip? And if he didn't, how did he think his picture related to that Jesus?

If our understanding of the gospels has been right, Jesus has to be projected as it were at two levels. The gospels present Jesus as he was seen and experienced as the Lord of the community brought into being by him. They looked at the figure of the past in the light of what they knew him now to be. For they knew that it was as the living Lord that he saves, as his earthly life is illuminated and given a new understanding by his whole career – by his whole ministry culminating in a cross, vindicated by a resurrection, and impregnated by the faith of a community who felt that they lived in the power of his immediate presence.

The life of Jesus itself was not the object of their faith. Indeed, of itself it could not sustain it for, to be viewed as saving, it had to be completed by, caught up in, the insight of those who lived in him. Yet they could not turn their backs upon the earthly life; neither the problems of the present nor the ambiguities of the life itself would allow them to do that. Their faith in him had to be justified by reference to his life.

Moreover, the life was needed to give reality to that present release which they experienced through him. They could accept his present Lordship as one which brought grace, freedom, and hope, only because these had already been discovered in his life. The Living Lord needed Jesus of Nazareth – Jesus, no one else, had to be Christ – to make belief in him an act of joy and real release.

The proclamation of the gospels is that it is the whole event of Jesus which saves. That is why Mark makes Jesus himself proclaim the gospel (1.15) which elsewhere, in Mark and beyond, is the whole Christian message of the life, redemptive death, and resurrected Lordship of Jesus. John presents Jesus in terms of the Lord he knows him now to be – though in fact, in the process he comes near to losing sight of the Jesus who was. Luke, who, because he also includes the Acts of the Apostles, has to be much more conscious of the gap between the time of Jesus and his own time, nevertheless, presents the ministry of Jesus as that of one who is progressing towards his Lordship, and he does so in such a way that the end infuses and controls the whole movement of getting there. Paul maintains that he is determined to look at Jesus, not just from an angle controlled by human evaluation, but from one decreed by an insight derived from belief (II Cor. 5.16).

The gospels – and the New Testament as a whole – proclaim Jesus of the past in the light of what they know him now to have become by virtue of their writers' place in the community which lives in response to him as it experiences his gracious presence in its members now. 'Jesus is Lord' – that credal statement meant that as they looked at Jesus, they saw him, not as he was, but as he had become for them now. His life was pictured in terms of the reality they now experienced in him. Nevertheless, it was the earthly life alone which enabled the present experience to be one of reality itself. What they now received as gracious arose out of the life even though it was not wholly contained by it.

Once it is accepted that our portrait of Jesus – the image we have of him and the vision we project of him – is not a photograph of his time on earth, once it is allowed that it has been infused with the responses of those who have later felt grasped by him, once it is seen that the Jesus of history is not to be identified with the Christ of faith – that the former relates to the latter as the part to the whole – then, the biggest danger facing us is perhaps that of forgetting Jesus of Nazareth altogether, of turning away from the historical figure who set it all in motion, and of concentrating wholly upon the person of the Lord. That does not in itself mean a neglect of the life, but rather entails a viewing of the life wholly in terms of the Lord we know him now to be. We let the ambiguities of history be dissolved in the setting of the faith.

It is I think a very real danger. A few years ago, I was taking a Lent course with a group of ordinands' wives under the general title, 'What Christians believe'. One of the sessions was concerned with Jesus during his time of earth – what he was like, what he taught, the claims he made, why he was crucified, and so on. In the course of the discussion I was somewhat startled when one of the wives loudly proclaimed that she was not at all interested in Jesus as he was: it was Jesus as he is now who was important to her – Jesus as he is found in the Christian community, in its worship, its sacraments, its creeds, and its scriptures. This was the Jesus who mattered; the other Jesus, Jesus as he actually was in his lifetime, was of little relevance and, anyway, did not engage her. She started with Jesus as she experienced him now and as that experience was illuminated by the experience of the Christian church, and informed by the past as it was enshrined in the creeds and in the gospels understood in their light.

I have to admit that I was somewhat taken back by this. I was pointing out the difference between Jesus as he appears to us and Jesus as he actually was in all probability in his time on earth, and was discussing the difficulty of getting back to a clear picture of him then, and here I found myself being outflanked by an easy acceptance of the differences and a willingness to let the Jesus of history go completely without any pangs or regrets. There is nothing quite so disconcerting to the self-styled radical as to be outflanked in this way and to be told that what he is suggesting as a difficulty has in fact already been faced and, indeed, that a solution has already been worked out! I was appearing to make heavy weather of a problem that had already been resolved on a basis of experience supplemented by commonsense!

Of course, for most of us it is the Christian community, of which we are a part and from which we inherit a common experience of Jesus as Lord and Christ, which really determines our understanding of what Christianity is, and we therefore see Jesus through eyes sharpened by its experience as well as our own. We find him in the community and in our individual life, and these two experiences mould our picture of him. What he was or what the Bible says he was is filtered through this experience and allowed, if not made, to fit it. Jesus as he was is taken up into the Christ and Lord he is for us, and the present experience determines how the picture of the past is received. Gathered round the Lord's table on the Lord's day we see him as he feeds the five thousand, not as

some royal messianic figure announcing the imminent arrival of the
kingdom of God and acting with such authority that the crowds were
impelled to seek to make him king. We do not even see him as a miraculous controller of natural things. Instead we see him as one who bestows
the bread of life as he comes now to feed and renew his followers, as the
one who makes God both real and gracious to us. The historian's questions about the original significance of the event pale into insignificance,
even into unreality, and the sceptic's questioning of the miraculous becomes totally beside the point. Who cares what did or did not, what
could or could not have happened nearly two thousand years ago? We
know what happens now, and we know the Jesus who is. And so, like
the ordinand's wife, we get impatient with the minutiae, with the dis-
sectors, with the probabilities and possibilities, with what it might or
might not have meant. The Jesus who is – the living Lord – is the one
who is important, and Jesus as he was is transposed quite easily if he
needs to be (though we don't usually see the need to think about it: it is
all quite spontaneous) to become one with what he is now. The past is
past: the present is all important.

And this, in one way at any rate, is quite right. We know Jesus as he
comes to us now, and this is the Jesus who saves. The Jesus of the past
must be caught up into the Lord of the present.

But he is not to be identified with him, as though he was always what
we know him now to be. The clear assertion of the New Testament as a
whole is that the resurrection advanced Jesus in some way, that it was
not merely the case of a new apprehension on the part of the disciples,
but that he actually assumed a new status at that point. During his time
on earth he is described either as not yet established in that relationship
with God that he was later to have by virtue of his exaltation, or – if the
imagery of pre-existence is used – he is regarded as either having re-
gained or advanced that status which had been voluntarily abandoned at
his incarnation. Only in John is this clear distinction blurred but even
there the prologue, by its assertion that 'the Word was made flesh', and
the Lord's talk to Mary of his Ascension, suggest that Jesus during his
time on earth was not identical with the Jesus of the exaltation. In practice, however, we do identify them. We think, teach and preach as
though Jesus during his time on earth was fully what we believe him
now to be. The risen Lord is in effect allowed to do a take-over of the
man who walked in Palestine.

And this outlook has a very real danger. In the first place, quite
simply, Christianity ceases to be a gospel when it is divorced from

history, and Jesus Christ ceases to be Christ when he is cut adrift from Jesus. The kerygma is the proclamation that God has acted and continues to act in the world and in people. It proclaims, not our search for God, but God's coming to us. The nature of that coming, the relationship that is forged between God and man, and the manner of God's initiative are all revealed in the life, death, and resurrection of Jesus of Nazareth. Jesus is the paradigm, not merely of man's faith in God, but also of God's grasp of men. The response witnesses to the life, and the life is needed to control, empower, and to correct the response.

Secondly, we need Jesus to pull our ideas of what Christianity is back to source and to keep our understanding in check. We need Jesus to stop Christ from becoming what in fact we think we need him to be rather than what he really is. Without a remembrance of Jesus as he was it is hard to see what can recall the church to her true stance, her true life-style – it is hard to see what can recall her to a true understanding of her nature and a true concern for her vocation when, as has happened so frequently over the years, she is in danger of forgetting this. Today is perhaps a time when appeal is too easily made to Jesus in an attempt to discover a simple faith or to back-up strivings which can all too easily degenerate into self-gratification. Nevertheless, this appeal to Jesus against the church is a valid one and must encourage the church herself to appeal to him and bring herself under the light of his judgment. 'What would Jesus have said about this, or felt about that?' is not a question which should be dismissed easily as naive, irrelevant, obtuse, or useless. 'What does his life suggest should be our response to this situation?' is a very necessary guide to our own outlook.[1]

Christianity cannot cut adrift from that figure of long ago without the danger of its becoming something other than it is legitimately meant to be. It must move on from that figure: there must be development from him, but it must be a question of unpacking the full significance of what is seen in him rather than an evolutionary movement which is impelled by its own momentum and which then can all too easily leave behind its beginnings to lose itself in something other than it really is. Christians must engage in a running battle with all that would cut them adrift from that enigmatic figure of long ago.[2]

So the preacher will not turn his back upon Jesus of Nazareth. Though he will aim to bring his congregation into relationship with the living Lord and will preach Jesus as he is known and accepted within the faith of the believing community, he will know both that this is achieved only when the Lord is seen to be continuous with Jesus of

Nazareth, and also that he can only really be Christ who is received as informed and controlled by him. We need Jesus as he was to make us open to the Lord and Christ he can be.

We shall bear in mind the urgency of Jesus' summons to discipleship and the total demand that his followers should take up the cross for themselves. We shall remember his proclamation of the kingdom of God which had a much wider significance than the one which envisages the incorporation of men into a church. We shall point out that he sat light to the things of this world and that his teachings and his actions totally reversed its values. We shall rejoice in his free acceptance of all who sought him out, whatever their need and however imperfectly it was expressed. We shall not fail to acknowledge that his challenge to estab-lished values and his openness to all issued in a commitment and a message which was truly radical in that it went right to the heart of things and turned outlooks, attitudes, expectations, and standards upside down. He was crucified because he was a threat to his contemporaries – religious and otherwise – and because his demand was too uncomfort-able, because, whilst he demanded so much of some, he received others so freely. He therefore left no cause for satisfaction, no room for pride of any kind. He refused to be compartmentalized and his followers were themselves therefore to seek neither security nor satisfaction in a status which the world could easily recognize and acknowledge. They like him were to be such an irritant to others that it would inevitably entail crucifixion for themselves.

These things are clear and must be a part of any picture of Jesus that emerges. As such they offer both powerful content to our preaching and compelling judgment upon our discipleship. It is when we try to go beyond them and to seek for the unifying factor behind Jesus – to find as it were what made him tick – that we come into difficulties. Over the centuries Jesus has been portrayed in a bewildering variety of guises, and this is not so much the result of perversity or obscurantism on the part of those who sought to discover who he really was as an inevitability brought about both by the nature of our sources and by the person of the man himself.[3]

There are in fact two difficulties which blight our search for Jesus. The first is one which is largely of our own making. We want to arrive at a figure who is easily embraced by us. In one form of his desire we want him to be easily identified as the Lord we believe him now to be – to be a full and complete manifestation of the proclamation of the church, to be obviously capable of bearing the full weight of the creeds, of being universalized in the kerygma. If we don't hanker after that, if we look more for the human Jesus, then we tend to want him to be immediately appealing as a person to us, one who invites an immediate response, who is immediately worthy of our devotion and who strikes chords in us 'deep down'. Either way – whether it be that which approaches him in the first place by way of his divinity, or that which on the other hand comes to grips with him by way of his humanity – either way we want a Jesus who is immediately, compellingly, and obviously worthy of our allegiance. We want him to be one with us – so that even his judgment of us is one to which we can consent. In short, we want a Jesus who is immediately intelligible to us in the twentieth century.

And the hard fact is that he isn't. It is a salutary exercise to try to commend Jesus to a group of modern schoolchildren. He does not come over as a figure who makes an obvious appeal. Whilst his abandonment of concern for the things of this world might commend him to a particular type of teenager, to others that same characteristic comes over as total irresponsibility. It appears as an opting out from the legitimate claims of the world. Whilst from one angle his whole-hearted commitment, his conviction, his no-nonsense approach strikes chords with some, it earns the rebuke of intolerance and arrogance from others who see him riding rough-shod over his opponents with scant respect for their outlook and little understanding of their positions.

And so we could go on, but the fact is that while he appeals to a certain spectrum of rather idealistic youngsters, he seems to offend the practical, the down-to-earth, and the sensitive; whilst he commends himself to a starry-eyed Malcolm Muggeridge, he offends a Bertrand Russell who puts a far higher value upon the attitude and outlook of one such as Socrates.

When Jesus is so presented as to make a direct appeal to us, there is almost certainly a partiality, an incompleteness, a selectivity, about the presentation.[4] And the reason is not hard to see. Such pictures paint him, almost inevitably, as a modern man, as one who is one with us, and, in so doing, fail completely to account for the impact he made upon his contemporaries who were not twentieth-century idealists but first-century Jews, living in the first-century world, in first-century political conditions, and whose faith was formed against the background of Jewish belief and contemporary hopes. William Temple once remarked that it was almost inexplicable why anybody should have bothered to have crucified the Jesus of the many popular lives that were current in the nineteenth century. But the fact is that Jesus was crucified, and this came about not merely because he challenged the self-centredness and concern for self-preservation of the powers that be, but because, in the doing, he made great claims for himself which his life and manner belied. His Jewish opponents were not all the hypocritical schemers, seeing in him a threat to their own established order, that we invariably picture them as being. They were probably no better and no worse than the church of our day. They disposed of Jesus because he was a false pretender. What by his actions and his teaching he claimed to be – to be one with and the means of God's final saving activity – was belied by his situation. He was a danger, a scandal, a threat. He claimed to override the covenant that God had established, and he gave no real sign that his claims were true. Otto Betz, in his study of the Jesus of history, no doubt puts his finger on the right point when he says in relation to the trial of Jesus: 'Anyone who claims the Messianic dignity must consider that according to scripture he must also be "Son of the Blessed" – the son of God. It is not only his own honour, it is the honour of God that is at stake. A powerless person who maintains that he is the Messiah blasphemes Almighty God, and in the eyes of the Jews blasphemy is the worst of all crimes.'[5] Jesus to his contemporaries would not have seemed that pillar of sweet reasonableness and obvious truth that we tend to make him. His claims were such that he, to them at least, was a fraud.

And it is in fact those claims – that drawing of attention to himself which overrides his opponents – which leave their mark on those who find him unattractive. There is an offence about the real Jesus of history which is itself timeless. Failure to leave room for that offence is to reduce him, to avoid the enigma, and to smooth the stumblingblock. We tend to go round it rather than to face it, by making him into an example of what seems to us to be virtuous action. But, he worked out his mission, he worked out his understanding of his vocation, in dialogue with the beliefs of his contemporaries, and in so doing challenged those beliefs at their most significant points. His offence was intelligible to them and it was real for it was made in terms of the messianic and apocalyptic expectations of his day.

If that is the first hindrance to our preaching the real Jesus of Nazareth – our desire to accommodate him to the beliefs or outlook of ourselves rather than to accept that he was a first-century man who engaged in an intelligible conflict with his contemporaries – the second arises from the nature of the sources which are available to us for a reconstruction of him. The gospels are not biographies and they do not give us an easy way into his thinking, his development, or his inner beliefs. Such things do not seem to have interested the evangelists for they were concerned primarily with the present rather than with the past. They therefore did not set out to answer the questions that we are now asking. We face a real problem here. We cannot ignore it for it is not of our making. Nevertheless, even though they offer us a Jesus as he was understood in the light of their faith, we can still use the gospels to come to a genuine insight into the way Jesus went about his task and so to some real understanding of how he thought about himself. The evidence has to be of an indirect nature. Particular details, particular events, even particular pieces of teaching have to be used with caution, but when the gospel accounts are taken as a whole, when one as it were steps back from the individual narratives to view the overall sweep, direction, and atmosphere, then one can arrive at a picture which gives an adequate statement of him and one which is of such a kind as to account, in the light of the resurrection experience, for the early church's response to him. Such an approach allows two factors to stand out clearly, namely, Jesus' radical stance and his assertion of the coming of the kingdom of God.

These two points must be at the heart of our preaching of him, and these must be seen in the light of that further point on which we have been insisting, namely that Jesus lived, worked, and died as a first-century man, and expressed his ideas through terms which were intelligible to, and which he really shared with, his contemporaries. When this is done, it has two effects upon our preaching of him, one of which is immediately helpful to us as we proclaim him within the context of the believing community, and one which though equally necessary, is much less obviously so.

The first result is to bring Jesus closer to the Christian response and to declare inadequate those estimates of him which would approach him, either within or without the church, as simpler, as making less complicated claims for himself, and so as demanding a less dogmatic response than that made by the Christian community. We might applaud Don Cupitt's desire as expressed on television to 'bring back Jesus and Jesus' message of the kingdom of God and locate ideas of faith, grace, etc. in his life'. That is a wholly necessary concern if the church is not to let the Christ of faith become a myth and a product of wishful-thinking. The modern recovery of Jesus has, however, discovered one who was by no means simple in his appeal or undogmatic in his demands.

The 'New Quest of the Historical Jesus', as it is usually called, has left us in no doubt as to the inadequacy of that older, liberal, quest which resulted in a picture of him as a preacher proclaiming the fatherhood of God and the infinite value of the human soul. No less rigorous in its approach to the gospels, it nevertheless takes the whole of their witness into consideration and, when it does, it arrives at a picture of a Jesus who was both far more radical and also far more self-assertive than the more liberal lives allowed. Jesus comes across as a person claiming total authority and so coming before his contemporaries as compelling a decision for or against himself. He was a self-assertive figure, who made total and unrestricted claims for himself. This is seen, not so much in the titles which are used, for these have fairly obviously received attention from the early church, but in what may be termed the more indirect evidence which comes across loud and clear and which offers a much firmer basis for assessing his self-understanding.

Jesus' use of titles remains unclear. There is very little evidence to suggest that he called himself Son of God and whether he thought of himself as Messiah remains open to doubt. He certainly did not go out of his way to encourage its application to him, but he did not actually forbid its use when Peter blurted it out, and (unless the synoptic account of an entry into Jerusalem is totally untrue to the original event) he equally certainly did not go out of his way to foreclose on such speculation. Before the highpriest he seemed to acknowledge that the dignity pertaining to such a title was not above him even though he quickly turned it aside in favour of that of Son of Man. This seems to have been his chosen self-designation, and the fact that it soon disappeared suggests that it really was remembered as his own witness to himself. Just what he meant by it though is one of the most vexed questions of New Testament scholarship, and this is no doubt caused fundamentally, not by undue scepticism, but by the nature of our sources and by the different ways in which they handle the term as well as by the actual difficulties in knowing what it would have conveyed to his contemporaries.[6]

So then, it is the indirect witness of Jesus to himself which needs to be taken seriously and, when this is done, it is seen to be very strong indeed. Jesus confronted his contemporaries with an authority and therefore with a demand which comes legitimately only from one who believed that God had committed to himself something which by right was his alone, and he met men with a grace which again could be exercised legitimately only by one who felt wholly united to God and to his final purposes for men.[7]

Two things in particular show the authority and therefore the demand of Jesus. There is, first, his attitude to the law. Jesus dared to place himself over and against the law of Moses, not in the manner of one who stood in total opposition to it, but in that of the more devastating critic who, while accepting its basic tenets and goodness, nevertheless deepened what it proclaimed where its demands were deemed to be inadequate, and actually overruled it where its requirements were seen to be either secondary or even wrong.

His 'But I say unto you', whilst not necessarily actually criticizing the limitations of the old law, nevertheless pointed out that they were in fact limitations, and proclaimed a demand which was appropriate to a new time which presented man with the nearer presence of God. The law had to give way before him who was the Sabbath's lord and the law's fulfilment. Jesus demanded a new attitude of all men, and it was the publican who repented who was justified rather than the Pharisee whose keeping of the law blocked the recognition of his need of God's grace, and so of his need of Jesus. Jesus required more than the keeping of the law; at the same time, however, no law at all could guarantee that one was right with God, for the Sermon on the Mount is no set of new regulations capable of being fulfilled, at least in this world as it is. Jesus threw men back to living by grace, and his demand was a proclamation that such grace could be found only by surrender to him. As he said to the rich man who kept the law: 'You lack one thing; go, sell what you have, and give to the poor, and you will have treasure in heaven; and come, follow me.' Of Jesus and the law, Ernst Käsemann has well written: 'Jesus felt himself in a position to override, with an unparalleled and sovereign freedom, the words of the Torah and the authority of Moses.' 'The Jew who does what is done here has cut himself off from the community of Judaism – or else he brings the Messianic Torah and is therefore the Messiah.'[8] Jesus proclaimed nothing less than a new approach of God and a new way to him. Both God's new approach and the new way to him were being made through himself alone. If the law could not serve the new, it had to go.

The authority and therefore the total demand of Jesus are seen, secondly, in the parables which formed such a distinctive part of his teaching. Here modern scholarship has helped enormously, for it has rescued the parables on the one hand from the straitjacket imposed upon them by an artificial and over-subtle allegorical exegesis which hid their directness and simplicity and, on the other, from the vague moral generalizations which turned them into innocuous and sentimental expositions of the love of God and the brotherhood of men. Both these methods dulled their impact and detached them from the person of Jesus himself. If C. H. Dodd[9] placed them firmly within the context of Jesus' life and related them wholly to his overriding message of the immediacy of the kingdom of God, so that they appeared as closely related to the person of Jesus, more recent scholarship has gone even further to unpack the stark quality of their message and to make them into the means of an actual encounter with the immediate presence of God through him.

They are now seen for what they are, as real, vital, compelling addresses where the word meets the listener in an actual event which means that he is left in some way different from what he was before. The situation in the parable stands in stark contrast to that in which the listener is involved and it demands a decision which calls him out from his context and imposes a demand for the complete reversal of his way. The parable opens up a new possibility and compels a decision for or against what it proclaims.[10]

In this sense the parable is a real word-event which forces itself upon the listener and inevitably moves or hardens him. For the parable contains within itself the action of God to which it witnesses. It is itself a direct confrontation and a compelling action. When Nathan faced David with the parable of the seized ewe-lamb (II Sam. 12.1–9), it moved him by its power and, with Nathan's 'Thou art the man', convicted him in such a way that no escape from its message was possible. Of itself, it either restored or condemned him. It created the crisis that the entry of God required and, by so doing, enabled the action of God to take place. Jesus' parables did precisely the same thing, but now they pointed always to the action of God in him.

For Jesus is himself a part of God's End-time. His parables proclaim that the kingdom is present in him, however hidden it may be and however much it is in the present to be contrasted with its future revelation. Jesus is one with the kingdom; he is wholly of it and united to it. Parables like that of the Prodigal Son, and the more obviously parables of the kingdom like that of the Great Supper, argue from the ministry of Jesus and his own action in receiving sinners and eating with them to the God who is behind him. From his own actions he determines and justifies God's actions – not the other way round which is the mark of the prophet. His ministry is itself part of God's final saving action, and when he is attacked, he argues from his ministry to that new action of God which is actually seen in him. It is an incredible attitude and can derive only from one who believes that God is totally committed to him.

His actions represent the novelty of God's actions, and God's will can be read off wholly from them. He is himself effectively standing in God's place. To reject him is to reject God; to receive him is a guarantee of God's acceptance. He does not proclaim the judgment of God; he brings it.

The parables are christological statements through and through. This is something that we must underline if we are to proclaim Jesus effectively. Our very familiarity with them has certainly dulled our appreciation of them for it has lessened their impact to such an extent that it is almost impossible for us to see their radical nature and so to understand the offence they caused to their original hearers. Thus, for instance, we miss the real scandal inherent in the parable of the Pharisee and the Tax-collector. We get used to the idea that the Pharisee was a hypocrite and so we accept the justice of the outcome. But this is reading it through our (not unbiased) eyes. For the original hearers, however, the Pharisees were no such thing; they represented the best of the piety of the Old Covenant. To them therefore, Jesus' proclamation was nothing less than offence, for it turned the old order upside-down and, by seeing the parable within the context of his own ministry, made total claims for himself.

But if Jesus met men with the final demand of God, he met them also with the fullness of God's grace. He taught men to call God 'Abba', 'Father', and he could do so only because he himself was conscious of his own Sonship from which that of others could be derived and in virtue of which they could claim their new status. He could mediate such a relationship to them because it could be guaranteed by his own unmediated Sonship. His characteristic way of addressing God was that of 'Father'.[11] Jesus regularly and naturally, addressed God as 'Abba' and this therefore set him apart from his Jewish contemporaries who would have understood that mode of address to be shockingly over-familiar and lacking in reverence.

Again, it is easy for us as twentieth-century Christians to overlook the significance of this. Jesus' attitude to God was an offence to his religious contemporaries for it seemed to belittle God's holiness. But Jesus taught that God's glory is revealed, not in his apartness, but in his oneness with men, and is seen supremely in his acceptance of them. Jesus' God was a prodigal God, one who appeared to waste his gifts and who seemed wholly insensitive as to the real nature of those on whom he bestowed them. To his contemporaries Jesus was in danger of destroying God. On the other hand, the graciousness of his God was not found in

an easy-going relationship – that is just the sentimentality and super-
ficiality of our modern outlook. His God's graciousness was found in an
offensive removal of all barriers, in a positive movement towards the
outcast, in a total and unreserved acceptance of them. It left no room
for superiority of any kind – even of that kind which reveals itself in the
somewhat false mateyness of so many modern religious exercises. It was
much more demanding, much more embracing, much less discriminating, and therefore much more radical than that. It just accepted the
unacceptable, and that meant that no one could glory in, or even feel
cosily assured by, acceptance. Jesus' acceptance of all was singularly
discomforting.

For Jesus received sinners and ate with them. This was the ultimate
sign of his confidence, as well as the ultimate offence to his contemporaries, for it meant that it put no bounds around the disposal of God's
grace. 'Now the tax-collectors and sinners were all drawing near to hear
him. And the Pharisees and Scribes murmered, saying, "This man
receives sinners and eats with them".' Like all the meals in the gospels,
these meals have a strong eschatological significance, that is, they look
forward to and in some way anticipate the banquet of the kingdom of
God. Jesus often refers to this future meal: 'Many will come from east
and west and sit at table with Abraham, Isaac, and Jacob in the kingdom
of heaven, whilst the sons of the Kingdom will be thrown into outer
darkness.' In Jesus, the final banquet is foreshadowed, and reception by
Jesus means that men are already being assured of their final place.
Jesus therefore did not prepare men for the kingdom; he received them
into it. His role was not preparatory but anticipatory. There was a unity
between what was happening in his ministry and what was to happen at
the end. That unity was such as to make the two parts cohere in a single
whole.

This leads us into the second effect that a concern with the Jesus of
history should have upon our preaching, and this time it is one which
isn't easily assimilated by us. It arises out of our realization both that
Jesus made very great claims for himself – that he was wholly one with
God's final and complete saving action – and also that he expressed this
self-understanding in terms compatible with his being a real first-
century man living among first-century men.

The synoptic gospels assert that Jesus' message was centred in an
expectation of the coming of the kingdom of God. As Mark summarizes
it, 'the time is fulfilled and the kingdom of God is at hand' (1.15).
Jewish beliefs about the kingdom at the time of Jesus appear to have

taken on various forms. Common to all was an expectation of the final action of God, when God would establish his rule and would dwell with his people. Rabbinic hopes of a more gradual, less dramatically open event shaded into those of apocalyptic which anticipated a final, open, eruptive, act of God when his reign would be established in a realm where his power would be openly vindicated in a dramatic event which all would see. Where did Jesus stand within this spectrum of beliefs? What did he mean when he preached that the kingdom was at hand, and when he urged his followers to pray for its coming?[12]

On the one hand, he proclaimed that the kingdom of God was present in him – that in some way his presence and activity established it now in our midst. So he could see his miracles at witnessing to its existence as a present reality, 'If I by the finger of God cast out devils, then is the kingdom of God come upon you.' As we have seen, his meals anticipated the kingdom. Nevertheless, as an anticipation they looked forward to the kingdom's future open realization, and in his answer to the rich man, Jesus clearly equated the kingdom with his questioner's hope of eternal life. Many of the parables contrasted the beginnings of the kingdom as they existed in Jesus with this future, open greatness. This in Mark is seen as the mystery of the kingdom which is known only to the faithful (4.11). Jesus did not envisage the kingdom simply as the real but itself unseen reign of God in the lives of men or even in the world as a whole. He expected a final, dramatic, clear, open, vindication of God's power. 'For whoever is ashamed of me and of my words in this adulterous and sinful generation, of him will the Son of Man also be ashamed, when he comes in the glory of his Father with the Holy angels.' And he said to them, 'Truly I say to you, there are some standing here who will not taste death before they see the kingdom of God come with power' (Mark 8.38–9.1).

This future form of expectation has, indeed, often been denied to Jesus. That it is symbolic language expressing an imagery which could be contained in no other way has often been maintained.[13] However, the early church certainly did not take it in this way. It accepted that he taught that the appearing of the kingdom would be an event for all to see when the Son of Man would be revealed, when evil would be destroyed, and when the resurrection of the dead would take place. The present age would effectively be brought to an end; a new age, dramatically other than the present, would be established. There would be an open demonstration of God's power and a dramatic vindication of their faith. It is impossible to exhaust the meaning of such passages as

I Thessalonians 4 and I Corinthians 15 by treating them as imagery. The early church expected an event – an event in history and in time which would bring this world to an end and establish the new.

It is sometimes suggested that, though the early church expected an imminent end, it did so because it misunderstood Jesus and got him wrong. Jesus is thus rescued from association with the undesirable and less charitable of the New Testament expectations which are then thought to arise out of the limitations of first-century belief. This may in fact make him more accessible to our age, but it does so at an enormous price – that of making him alien to his own times and a total failure at communicating his innermost convictions to his contemporaries.

But there is in the gospels no suggestion that Jesus was using the language in any way other than its usual meaning. There is rather everything to suggest that he looked forward to a dramatic initiative on the part of God. His ethical teaching represents a standard that is only capable of full realization when God's power is itself fully manifested and when his followers are able to live in direct dependance upon the wholly available and completely unhindered grace of God. They are the ethics of the kingdom of God. Jesus himself talked little of mission and he said almost nothing about the future age of the Spirit. Indeed, the Holy Spirit has little place in his teaching. The parables advocate the dramatic nearness of the final vindication, and the Last Supper is seen as an anticipation and guarantee of it. Jesus' whole life suggests this and his teaching proclaims it.[14]

The real problem is that Jesus is represented as proclaiming the nearness of this new event – of maintaining that the kingdom would come in power in the lifetime of some of his contemporaries (Mark 9.1) and that the Son of Man would appear before the passing away of this generation (13.26). This expectation was not realized. Was Jesus then mistaken? Many suggestions have been made to support the view that he wasn't. So, the kingdom's coming with power is equated with the transfiguration, the resurrection, or with Pentecost – or perhaps even with the fall of Jerusalem and the consequent emergence of the universal mission. The generation in which the coming of the Son of Man will occur has been seen as this age, or that of the witnessing disciples, or even as that of the enemies of Jesus. Sometimes the near expectation has been limited to the preliminary signs rather than to the actual Parousia. At other times a less literal meaning has been given to the proclamation of the imminence of the Parousia.[15]

Comforting though all this might be theologically, it has little to commend it as an explanation of Jesus' own thinking and teaching which, as we have seen, does not as a whole envisage a long time between himself and the Parousia. Again, it involves the early church in a great misunderstanding which totally undermines the effectiveness of Jesus as it leaves him wholly out of touch with their thinking. It can only make him thoroughly incompetent and them incredibly uncomprehending. By introducing special pleading in an attempt to solve one dilemma, it raises another the consequences of which are no less far reaching.

We cannot escape the conclusion that Jesus proclaimed his belief in an early end, and that this belief – at least in the form in which he expressed it – was not realized. Here then is our problem. It cannot be avoided and its size is not to be underestimated for it seems to undermine the credibility of Jesus and so to destroy our claims on his behalf. It is not just a question of his being wrong on timing. That in itself could be accounted for by appealing to the prophetic shortening of perspective, by maintaining that conviction and certainty make the event so real and so much a part of the present that it appears imminent and can only be preached as such. But it is more than that, for it seems to threaten not just his foresight but his insight also. It concerns the nature of the promise with which he addressed his disciples, for it would make him put false hopes before them, false promises of vindication, false expectations of God's activity.

And it is this which brings us to the heart of the matter. If Jesus expected and promised an early Parousia, then it would seem that he had a false understanding of the nature of God's saving activity, and so a false understanding of God. He expected a dramatic, open, vindication by God – one which displayed his sovereignty in a massive act of power and judgment. Like the Psalmist, he expected a God who would come and scatter his enemies. Instead of that, there was a God who led him to a cross, raised him though in a hidden vindication, who lets the world go on, who is made to tolerate suffering and remain silent before evil.

Are the expectation and the actuality so far apart that they cannot be held together? Are we left in a position where we can do nothing other than share in Temple's pain when he said, 'If I thought Jesus expected an immediate catastrophe other than his own death and resurrection, I *think* I should have to renounce Christianity.'

It is important to remember that the church has always been as insistent on the Lord's full humanity quite as much as it has on the full divinity. The real humanity of Jesus cannot be laid aside for, if it is, the

Christian belief about the God who gives himself in love to men is undermined and the equally important belief about man which expresses itself in terms of optimistic reality and in hope of his future unity in love with God himself is left with no basis in fact. In Jesus, God is discovered and encountered in a life which was truly human. Perfect humanity means being fully human: it means working out a full and complete response to God in a life which is a real human life at a particular time and in a particular place. It means entering into the culture, outlook, relationships, imperfections, and limitations of a particular point in time and working through them to find the reality of God and a right response to him. Jesus in his life prayed to the Father. In that prayer and in the working out of its response is to be seen both humanity and divinity in him. But it had to be a genuine prayer and a real response. Otherwise, Jesus is separated from us in such a way that he ceases to be perfectly human.

Jesus was a genuine man of his age. He transcended the limitations that this put upon him, not by being apart from them, but by working through them. And he worked through them only by believing in them. And he could believe in them only by truly entering into them. As a man of his age, he could only express the certainty of his place as the final inaugurator of God's saving work in terms of a kingdom which was already dawning in his own life and which was to be manifested completely in the immediate future. Anything less would have made him claim nothing more than did John the Baptist. The reality of God's salvation in his own life meant that he was inextricably linked to the final kingdom, and the fullness of that link meant that the final revelation had of necessity to be expected soon. Given his Jewish background, given his present experience, given the expectations of his contemporaries, Jesus could have explained himself – to himself as well as to others – in no other way. Anything less would have caused them to accept him only as a prophet, merely as a precursor. He would not have made God real to them in the way that he did, and he would not have been accepted as that part of God's final act which he believed himself to be. Jesus had to authenticate himself to his contemporaries. It had to be a genuine authentication, one in which the external proclamation represented a true expression of what lay in the man himself. He had to work out his place in God's design in terms of the beliefs he shared with his contemporaries, and he had to do it because he really believed in what he was proclaiming.

Without this near-expectation, it is hard, if not impossible, to see how Jesus could have believed in himself or how his contemporaries could have been brought to believe in him.

Though this may lessen it, it still does not solve the problem of Jesus' apparent incomplete grasp of the hidden nature of God's saving act and so his incomplete understanding of God's nature – of his working within nature, of his limited power in the universe, and above all of his gentler dealings with man – that he does not appear for all his greatness as a judging God but as a receiving one.

And how do we know the truth of this latter assertion? Only of course because of the life of Jesus – of his acceptance of men, of his forgiving of them, of his entering upon the way of the cross, and of his willingness to go to it.

Actions speak louder than words, and it is in the actions of Jesus that God is revealed, for these express the depths of Jesus' being, they reveal his innermost nature, they uncover his true self. Here is both his spontaneity and also his most determined commitment.

If Jesus' ideas are expressed in the forms of his day, if they are shaped by the world-view in which he shared, if they are limited by his real part in the culture and beliefs of his time – if they are hemmed in at least in part by the age in which he lived – it is his actions through which his true self, his real being, is expressed and where he is enabled to break free and to transcend the limits of his real humanity.

By his life, Jesus rose above his own teaching; by his insight, he transcended his own expectations; by his own self-giving he shattered all bands, all limitations, all hindrances of the moment, to be one with God and so both to express and be God's saving act. We must let Jesus himself judge the adequacy of his words, and we must find his divinity in his total pursuit of God's will and in his total transcendence of the limitations that his humanity placed upon him. His obedience to what he saw to be the will of God made him one with God and resulted in a life which rose above the limitations placed upon it by his full sharing in the life of men.

And his real transcendence is seen above all in his journey to the cross, and it is this which the modern critical study of the gospels has done much to illuminate. As the gospels now stand, the cross is seen as the fore-ordained climax of Jesus' ministry. After the crisis of the Caesarea-Philippi encounter, Jesus goes on his way determined to die in an event which expresses the full thrust of God's purpose for him. 'And he began to teach that the Son of Man must suffer many things, and be rejected by the elders and the chief priests and the scribes, and be killed, and after three days rise again. And he said this plainly' (Mark 8.31–32). Though this represents a new stage in Jesus' ministry which now takes the form of a controlled movement towards Jerusalem, this acceptance of the inescapable necessity of the cross is represented, not as a new apprehension on the part of Jesus, but rather as the culmination of a path which had been determined by the beginnings of the public career as these were controlled by the baptism and temptation. So, right from the beginning, the gospels appear to proclaim that Jesus entered deliberately upon a ministry which took him inevitably to a cross which he accepted as a full and complete part of God's design for him and which he knew would lead on into a resurrection in which he would be vindicated.

Modern criticism, however, has challenged this picture at a number of points. In the first place, it has maintained that Mark's clear picture is not necessarily biographically controlled but is in large part to be accounted for by theological rather than strict biographical considerations. The clear emphasis upon the necessity of the cross which appears in the second half of the gospel may therefore be there more because of the evangelist's own teaching concerns rather than because it represents an actual record of what was uppermost in Jesus' mind at the time. Secondly, the very clear predictions of the events of the crucifixion and resurrection which are found in this section of the synoptic gospels seem to have been built up in the light of the events rather than to have been actual reports of Jesus' own words. It is not easy to understand either the anguish and doubts of Jesus himself or the total fear and incomprehension of the disciples at the time of the crucifixion if Jesus was as clear about his future as these verses suggest. Moreover, as they now stand, they appear in the various gospels in forms which fit that particular evangelist's actual reporting of the later events. This suggests that the evangelists themselves have a creative part in their composition.

The third point is perhaps the most persuasive of all and is of such a kind that its conclusions must be taken very seriously. As we saw above, the general belief that Jesus was clear about his vocation and the way in which it was to be fulfilled, rested primarily on the assertion that he saw himself as the Suffering Servant of Yahweh who, in fulfilment of the prophecy of Isaiah 53, was to give up his life at the hands of enemies in a death which, though in the eyes of men seemed to be shameful, was in effect redemptive of them and which would issue in a divine vindication of a resurrection event. This belief, it was thought, guided his whole ministry, and determined his expectations.[16]

However, such an estimate of Jesus' self-understanding has been questioned very widely, and, what must cause us to take this questioning very seriously indeed, is the fact that doubts have been raised, not merely by the more radical gospel critics, but also by those who take a far more cautious view of the gospel narratives and who are concerned by and large to argue for their overall historicity.

For the fact is that there is in the gospels very little reference to the Servant. There is only one quotation from Isaiah 53 on the lips of Jesus (Luke 22.37). We may see other allusions – for example in Mark 10.45, and in the words of Institution and in the saying of Mark 9.12 – but these can remain at best as only inferences by us, and ones for which there is very little evidence. All in all, there is just not the hard evidence for thinking that Jesus saw himself in Servant terms, and even less for maintaining that Servant imagery played a decisive part in his thinking.

Isaiah 53 is the only clear reference in the Old Testament to a death which has redemptive consequences, and when it is realized that this played but little part in the actual thinking of Jesus, his approach to Jerusalem and the reasons behind it are left much less explicit than they first appear to be. What we have in the gospels is seen to be influenced by a Christian understanding of the death of Jesus rather than an actual evaluation of what he himself said about it.[17]

Once again, the real significance of Jesus and his saving work is to be discovered in what he did rather than in what he said. His actions expressed what he was, and it is in these that his true nature is revealed. Jesus was less certain about his future than the gospels now suggest. His path was not crystal clear; the manner in which he was to respond to God's call was not completely worked out; the full nature of the demand laid upon him by God was not wholly understood by him. The way of the cross for him was not one which was entirely comprehended; its results were not completely foreseen. There was an inescapable 'must' behind his journey to Jerusalem, an inevitable sense of purpose about the way he took, an incontestible belief that God's will would be worked out there in a series of events where his own destiny would be fulfilled and God's call of him would be realized. But just what it meant for him, he did not see. That death was a real possibility could not be denied – the fates of some of the earlier prophets and of John the Baptist made it very likely that he would be called upon to face its ultimate demands. But Gethsemane reveals that he did not always regard it as inevitable, and the Markan cry from the cross – 'My God, my God, why hast thou forsaken me?' – shows that his relationship with God remained one of surrender and obedience rather than one of total understanding and certainty. His journey to the cross was one of faith rather than of sight, of real openness to whatever lay before him, of victory of total response over partial surrender and incomplete perception of its outcome. His was a real journey to a true cross – to a cross of which the reality is seen in its darkness and isolation.[18]

The cross of Jesus meant not only suffering and isolation, pain and death: his embrace of its call meant also doubt and uncertainty, frustration and despair. It meant following a way which obedience and conviction laid down but which faith alone could justify. He did not see completely where his path was leading him, and he could go forward only in trust that vindication would follow. Jesus did not see clearly just how his way would achieve God's purposes, and he could only trust that God was to be found in it. In short, his embrace of the cross was an act of real faith, in that it entailed a commitment which could not see clearly what was to be achieved through it, and a trust that could not guarantee its results. His faith did not protect him from uncertainty, doubt, and despair. His embrace of the cross was a real surrender – total and complete. The cross was a call to total giving, to total self-emptying, to total self-abandon. Its way was in truth that of 'casting bread upon the waters' in the faith that it would result in a gathering in due time.

Such was the way that Jesus walked, and such an attitude is demanded of us who would follow in his way. And it is a path which is not merely hard to follow; it is one which is hard even to proclaim. For it is a way which demands a total launching out into the deep. It is a way which not merely does not offer obvious results; it does not even guarantee them. It is a way which does not make its success clear; it is a way which cannot even guarantee its correctness. The way of the cross is the way of seeming uselessness for it offers no certainty of its vindication. Its effectiveness cannot be judged, and its results are rarely seen. Its pursuit cannot be openly justified, and its vindication can be a matter of faith alone. It must seem ineffective, and it must be no guarantee against despair. To the world (and to us when we are of the world) it must seem foolishness, and it will be despised (by us also when we share in the world's outlook) as weakness. It is a call to total abandonment of self, for it will leave the self with no justification for its actions and no guarantee of the rightness of its weakness. It is a call to go on in darkness, believing only that out of darkness alone will come light. Such was Jesus' way when he entered upon that of the cross, and such is Jesus' call to his church when he summons it to follow him. Indeed, it can be one with him only when it shares in the way of the cross, for the resurrection does not cancel out the cross as a past event but rather makes it present. For as St Paul says when he writes to the Philippians, the power of the resurrection is found in the disciple only when it unites him to the cross: 'For his sake I have suffered the loss of all things, and count them as refuse in order that I may gain Christ and be found in him . . . that I may know him and the power of his resurrection, and may share in his sufferings, becoming like him in his death, that if possible I may attain the resurrection from the dead.'

7

'We Have Seen His Glory'

We have been maintaining throughout these chapters that the gospels are most properly understood when they are accepted as responses to Jesus – to the Jesus of history as seen and believed in in the light of the resurrection and of the continuing experience of his lordship in the early church. They are proclamations of the evangelists to their contemporaries, and they express their convictions through the vehicle of the beliefs and thought-forms, of the world-view, of their day.

It is important that we should be consciously aware of this understanding of the nature of the gospels when we try to sit at their feet and, if not exactly to make the whole of their proclamation their own, at least to learn from them and to be enriched by their statement of what they know had happened in their midst. This awareness on our part is nowhere more important than when we come to interpret those sections which stand at the heart of their proclamations but which are not easily entered into by us today, namely the infancy narratives, the resurrection stories, and the various miracle accounts that are to be found in their writings.

Here, the differences between their outlook and ours are probably at their greatest, and this means that all possible care must be exercised by us if we are, in the first place, to come to a right appreciation of what the evangelists were saying through these episodes to their contemporaries and, then, if we are to go on to understand what they can say to us today, what in fact we are to put before our congregations for their life and their wholeness in Christian believing.

The question of the nature of the miraculous in these episodes must be faced firmly and squarely. It may indeed be right sometimes to meet the objections of the twentieth century to the miraculous with the retort 'too bad for modern man' and to see our present scepticism as part and parcel of our predicament and of our alienation from the things of the spirit. There is indeed genuine cause for complaint against those theologians who refuse to treat the possibility of the miraculous with the seriousness which the biblical narratives deserve. 'What happens now' is sometimes allowed too much say in determining 'What could have happened then'. In this way, the possibility of the miraculous is ruled out of all consideration of what can be accepted as historical events.

It is, of course, perfectly true that our experience in the present will inevitably, and by no means necessarily wrongly, affect our expectations from the past, and anything lying outside our experience will have to undergo a more rigorous historical test. But to deny the judgment 'historical' to events which cannot be explained wholly within our present understanding of this world seems totally arbitrary. We might be inclined to believe that the sun could not have stood still for Joshua and, since it would be relatively easy to explain the belief that it did out of early Israelite man's naive outlook and his known ability to see God's direct intervention in a multiplicity of events, both moral and immoral, we could as historians say that it is unlikely to have happened. Indeed, we might with justice stick our necks out and say that it did not happen. Yet it would be hard to deal in the same way with, say, the story of the raising of Lazarus. Instinct might make us say that it could not have happened. Our historical judgment of its possible setting in the life of Jesus and of John's handling of history might make us feel that it is unlikely to have happened. But we could not go on and say that it could not possibly be historical. It might have happened, and our judgment as historians would seem to have to be 'not proven' but equally 'not disproven', 'possible' even if 'not likely'. We cannot just rule it out of court though only faith will let us make a final, positive evaluation of it.

It is no part of our task, then, to reduce the miracles in the gospels just for the sake of modern man's squeamishness. Our criterion on this will be, not what modern man will take, but rather a rigorous attempt to come to a true understanding of what the gospels are actually asserting. It is the gospels themselves which can provide the best clue as to how their miraculous element should be viewed by us.

There is nevertheless a point at which modern man's instinct must be allowed to speak, and this is what may be termed his moral instinct, his sense of what is right, of what is legitimate, of what is appropriate to the God who stands behind Jesus of Nazareth. An instance from the Old Testament can illustrate this point. Over a number of years, it has fallen my lot to read at the Easter Ceremonies the great biblical passages which point to and which illustrate the nature of God's saving action in the resurrection of Jesus. One of these has always been the record of Israel's crossing of the Red Sea which climaxed with the ending of Exodus 14: 'Thus the Lord saved Israel that day from the hand of the Egyptians: and Israel saw the Egyptians dead upon the seashore. And Israel saw the great work which the Lord did against the Egyptians, and the people feared the Lord; and they believed in the Lord and in his servant Moses . . . Thanks be to God.' This has always seemed to me a singularly inappropriate ending for a reading which was to be appropriated by Christians commemorating the resurrection of Jesus. It not only verbalized a vindictive delight in the congregational response but also a vindictive act on the part of God himself and, by its belief in the demonstration of open power, propounded something which was completely contrary to the hidden nature of the resurrection vindication. The miraculous here just had to be other than that suggested by the biblical response, for the nature of Jesus himself passed judgment upon the Old Testament understanding revealed in the Exodus proclamation. I would not have wanted an enquirer into Christianity to have overheard my reading and apparent acceptance of the biblical estimate of the event. Our scepticism about even some of the New Testament miracles is not always just a question of an unwillingness to believe in the supernatural. Often it is one rather of the near irrelevance of the miraculous, sometimes, indeed, almost of its absurdity. We might at least see the point of Jesus' stilling of the storm even though we might find its actual happening hard to believe, but what is the point – as far as we can see it – of his walking on the water? What was Jesus trying to do or to prove? If it is a question of the miraculous here then for us the major stumbling-block may well be its extravagence, its prodigality, its unnecessarily open display of divine power which seems so alien to Jesus' usual way of life. Stories of the risen Jesus' eating before the disciples and of his showing to them the marks of the crucifixion do nothing to convince us of the reality of his resurrection. Indeed, if anything, they present us with extra, and often unnecessary, problems. Even the story of the virgin birth can add little to the actual significance of God's creative act in Jesus for those who no longer think in terms of the initial creation of man in a literal Adam.

The miraculous often presents a problem, not merely to our sense of the possible but, more seriously to our feeling of what is appropriate, even legitimate, to our understanding of what is right or worthy of credence. John and his readers might have been impressed by the raising of Lazarus, but we for our part find something almost objectionable in

Jesus' delay in going to the help of his friends and in his allowing Lazarus therefore to undergo the traumatic experience of physical death. Like the Lazarus of the modern poet, our Lazarus would have found the whole experience completely shattering, almost depersonalizing, and we may well baulk at Jesus' seeming overbearing use of an individual in order to make a point about his own significance and work.

At other times the miraculous can seem almost absurd. It is my custom every year just before Easter to get the youngsters at a local secondary modern school where I do some teaching, to read through – without any comment or exhortation from me – St Luke's account of the Passion. This almost invariably makes a considerable impact upon them. There is something here which seems to reach out and to engage even the most hard-headed sceptic among them. It is certainly an illustration of the power of the cross to move and to appeal. Yet, invariably again, the whole impact is almost lost by one incident – that of Jesus' healing of the high-priest's servant whose ear had been cut off by one of rhe Lord's followers. One can sense the feeling of incredulity that goes tound the room, and this, I am certain, is caused not so much by an unwillingness to believe in miracle as such, as by the way the children's minds boggle at what they are being asked to believe took place – the regrowth or return of the ear – and by the near sense of outrage at the littleness, even pettiness, of the whole episode. Surely Jesus could have stopped the incident from happening. Surely his moral stature could have restrained his followers. What enobled Jesus in the eyes of Luke and, presumably, in those of Luke's readers, plainly does the reverse to twentieth-century schoolchildren and, on this point at any rate, there is no doubt as to which is the right response.

If they are to move him to wonder and to an acknowledgment of divinity, modern man rightly makes of the miracles more demands than did his first-century predecessors. Luke alone records a miracle at this point. It had great significance for him, and the absence of it from both Matthew and Mark suggests that it was most likely his own addition to the story – that he added it as a further illustration of the peacefulness and innocence of Jesus. Its significance for him was wholly other than that which it has for our contemporaries, and is of such a kind as to suggest that he could well have added it to his Markan source purely out of a sense of what was appropriate to the Jesus he followed and therefore as what he imagined Jesus 'must' have done at this point in time.

Clearly we are in another world from that of the evangelists and their readers. We don't at all react in the same way as they did. What was compelling, thought-provoking, faith-inducing to them often seems just the opposite to us. The form in which their proclamation is contained cannot just be transferred to our age and be expected then to proclaim a message similar to that which it announced to them. Its impact is either dulled or distorted. It ceases to be a vehicle for announcing the good news as they saw it. It may be that in the end we will want to reject their proclamation, either in our rejection of Christianity as such or of Christianity as they understood it. To hear their proclamation doesn't necessarily mean that we will want to accept it. It may need correcting, enlarging, and freeing from the limitations of their age. For it must be remembered that if our age has a prejudice against the miraculous which must be countered in our attempts to say what was really going on behind the form of the biblical narratives, first-century man was equally strongly prejudiced in favour of them. He wanted them, expected them, needed them. For him they were the most natural thing in the world and he could confidently be expected to 'see' them, and so to write up his stories in their terms, where we could equally confidently be expected to see none. It is therefore vital that we should approach the gospels at these points as expressions of what was 'seen' to have happened by men who lived with first-century expectations and beliefs. In this way we shall have some chance of arriving at the true significance of what they were trying to say and so give their message a chance of impinging upon us to inform and deepen our own. It is the proclamation of the evangelists in these crucial areas that we are now to try to unravel. That unravelling will help us to decide how we are to preach these things to our congregations. In particular, it will ensure that we claim neither too little nor too much for them.

The Infancy Narratives

Christmas presents any parish priest with real problems. On the one hand there is the fact of the wide response to the proclamation of the birth of Jesus. On the other hand, there is the equally obvious fact that the response does not seem to go deep. It does not seem really to impinge upon the lives of those who come to our churches at Christmas – or, if that seems too judgmental an attitude, at any rate to be a lasting means of their being touched by the real proclamation of the Christ. The response as a whole seems to be superficial, the product of a hangover of the balmy days of folk-religion, an attitude that is in real danger of merging into the sentimental.

Yet, the very fact of Jesus himself warns us that we must not despise such a response – that we must neither look down nor turn our backs upon a glimmer of the truth however dim it be, that we must not turn away from a partial surrender, from a witness to a need however barely it is felt and however imperfectly it is expressed. It would be easy to be dismissive, just as it would be easy to acquiesce in the response and to use it as part of our self-gratification.

We cannot be dismissive of the wide response to the Christmas story as this is expressed in the large congregations at our carol services and midnight eucharists. These can in fact help to bring out the best in men and to be an expression of the greatness of human love, of the worth of the family, of the hope for better things, even of a momentary glimpse of wonder and of awe which can contribute so much to the quality of man's god-given life. The trouble is, though, that it is in the end all so very temporary. It barely survives the post-Christmas blues. It doesn't really bridge the gap between December and January. It succeeds in expressing and in part sanctifying what good there already is in the hearts of men rather than in deepening that by causing it to be seen in its true light and by bringing to bear upon it the quickening, but chastening, love of God.

Undoubtedly, one of the reasons for this is the fact that Christmas itself is geared around the Christmas narratives, seen as stories rather than around the real beliefs behind those stories. And when the infancy narratives are taken primarily as story, their ability to move, their power to be a vehicle of Christian proclamation is limited in the extreme. For as story they stand alone, divorced from the life of Jesus and from the beliefs of the early Christian community about him. However reverently they are told, however much something of the wonder of life comes across in some of the actors in our infants' nativity plays, when they remain at the level of story their power to move is not strong and their ability to summon out a genuine Christian response to the one who is there proclaimed is minimal.

And this, of course, should not be a matter for surprise. The infancy narratives are amongst the latest of our gospel records and, of them-selves, they can add little to their proclamations. What they do is to sum up, express, and even justify, the proclamation of the whole of the evangelists' gospels. Without the narratives that follow them, and the beliefs that these unfold, indeed without the community witness that these proclaim, they can express little. It is therefore not surprising if their impact upon those who are unwilling to link them to the challenge of the whole of the gospels they introduce is minimal. They look at the infancy of Jesus in the light of the whole of his life as it includes his death, resurrection, and continuing presence in the Christian community. Devoid of that dimension, they can be little more than tales of a past event which cannot have much of an abiding significance for the present. They express a faith and, taken alone, are not themselves vehicles for promoting faith. It is therefore as expressions of faith that they must be proclaimed.

And the trouble is that they do not any longer really come over as expressions of faith. They no longer shout out a proclamation that 'God was in Christ reconciling the world to himself'. They no longer sum up the whole work of God in Jesus.

Now this may be simply a part of modern man's divorce from the things of God. It may be just a part of his unwillingness to subject himself to the searching glance of the divine; it may be just a part of his search for self-sufficiency and independence. Yet the true situation may not be quite as simple as that suggests. For this relegation of the infancy narratives into the realm of story, this distancing of them from us by transferring them into the sphere of the sentimental, of the unreal, of the world of legend, fairy-story, and popular tale may be because there is in fact in them something of a built-in obstacle to treating them as real history. Our present instinct tells us that they are not hard and fast accounts of events that actually happened. Angels do not come to earth or appear as choristers from the skies. People do not speak such poetic masterpieces. Wise men do not travel in state yet make visits to obscure houses whilst contriving to keep such visits hidden from the local ruler. Stars do not move to stay over houses as some form of divine pointer. There is something unreal about these stories when they are taken as hard facts, and this makes them fit neither into modern man's understanding of reality, nor indeed into the life of Jesus itself. And so the twentieth century transfers them – either consciously or subconsciously – into the realm of story, of imagination, of idealism, of poetry, of the unreal, of the fairy-tale, and lets them express its own sentiments as these are awakened by the annual festival of the family, of man's goodwill to men.

And the point for us to notice is that modern man's instinct here comes close to what theologians have been saying for a number of years.[1] The instinct of modern man which feels that real history is not to be found in these narratives comes close to the conclusions on this point reached by many a sensitive and devout Christian seeker after truth.

What are the grounds which force the biblical critic to such a conclusion?

Some would be moved by the different atmosphere which pervades these stories as compared with that in the rest of the gospel narratives. Angels, dreams, moving stars, opening heavens, inspirational witness, babes leaping in the womb – all these taken together set them apart from the more sober realism of the later gospel narratives and link them much more closely to the legendary and to the folk-tales of other peoples. There is no real link between them and the later history of Jesus. Their events are never referred to later in the gospels and they seem to have left no impression either upon Jesus' contemporaries or, more importantly, upon Mary and the rest of Jesus' family.

However, the real reason for doubting that they are records of historical facts about Jesus' earthly beginnings is the differences between the accounts of these as they are found in Matthew and in Luke. For, quite apart from the difficulties in the individual stories, the biggest challenge to the historicity of the infancy narratives as a whole comes from the fact, not only that Matthew and Luke have two entirely different accounts, but also from the realization that their stories contain definite points of conflict. Both have Jesus born at Bethlehem, but is the Holy Family's residence there of long-standing (Matthew) or only temporary (Luke)? Both witness to a virgin birth, but is the revelation of this fact given to Joseph (Matthew) or to Mary (Luke)? Attempts to harmonize these two accounts by suggesting that the appearance of the angel to Joseph is not to inform him of the virginal conception but to persuade him to take Mary as his wife come to grief on the fact that the angelic message is plainly first and foremost an announcement of the conception by the Spirit. It is the knowledge of this which will calm Joseph's fears and so enable him to play his part in the divine plan. Any other interpretation seems to be of the nature of special pleading. Both gospels cause Jesus to be acknowledged by visitors, but are these shepherds at the manger or wise men at the house? Luke's Holy Family would have 'returned into Galilee, to their own city Nazareth' long before Matthew's wise men could possibly have arrived at Bethlehem. So Luke would have had no room in his time chart for the flight into Egypt, and he could not have allowed that the Holy Family may have contemplated remaining permanently in Bethlehem. For him, Nazareth was their 'own city' not a haven and refuge from the younger Herod lest he should prove to be something of a chip off the old block!

The two narratives just do not fit together and they can be made to do so only by ignoring the clear meaning of individual parts of the separate stories. That outlook which would see both as factual reports of real events and which would attribute Matthew's account to Joseph and Luke's to Mary is not really supported by either of the two narratives. It is an attempt to explain the different leading figures in the two stories but it remains inconceivable that either Mary or Joseph would have told such incomplete narratives and ones which completely excluded the part played by the other partner.

The difficulties therefore have to be faced and their true nature accepted. What though is their significance? A large number of conservative critics, faced with the reality of the differences and with the impossibility of harmonization without projecting something like a second visit to Bethlehem which then becomes the occasion of Matthew's events, cut their losses and solve the problem by abandoning Matthew in favour of Luke. Matthew's is then accepted as a popular and imaginative narrative based on Old Testament prefigurations and community piety.[2] Yet this solution has its own difficulties. Matthew's gospel as a whole is certainly not less historically oriented than is Luke's – indeed a strong case could be made out for precisely the opposite contention – and there is no hint that he is taking a different line in his first two chapters. He is certainly arguing a case – one that is based precisely on the fact that Jesus fulfilled Old Testament expectations, and his whole argument would have gone by the board if he had not believed that his events had actually happened. He may have got his history wrong, but it is quite illegitimate to assume therefore that he was not really intending to write history. As we have seen earlier, the real problem for us is that the evangelists' idea of history writing and ours do not really coincide.

Luke and Matthew cannot be divided in this manner. For Luke's story itself presents insoluble problems if it is to be taken as 'hard' history.[3] The Annunciation scene can only be accepted thus if Mary's answer to the angel is taken either as a misunderstanding of his salutation so as to make it either an announcement of an imminent birth or a recording of her pledge of perpetual virginity. Most commentators seem to prefer the latter explanation but there is really no evidence for it and it certainly does not arise out of the narrative itself. Luke's narrative, like that of Matthew, must in fact be accepted as imaginative reconstruction based on church tradition (which may or may not itself be based on solid evidence), on artistic concerns, on the art of sympathetic storytelling, but above all on the desire to make the story a vehicle for theological truth. From somewhere Luke has received the tradition of the virgin birth and he writes up the story to come to its dramatic climax:

> The Holy Spirit will come upon you,
>   And the power of the Most High will overshadow you;
> therefore the child to be born will be called holy –
>   the Son of God.

The Spirit of prophecy is at work in the characters of the infancy narratives. John, the supreme prophet, is Spirit-filled from the womb. Jesus, the saviour for whom John is but the precursor, is actually conceived through the Spirit. God is totally committed to him as he is himself the total saving action of God. The story of the annunciation is fashioned by Luke to make this dramatically clear. The narrative is history freely told in the service of theology.[4]

But how free is the telling? How far has the story taken over so that the history is obscured, if not submerged, as the narrative is moulded by insights of belief to become the vehicle of theological concerns? How far are the manger, the shepherds, the census, the ancient witnesses in the temple real events and how far are they theological proclamation? Such a question cannot be ignored even if in the end there is little chance of getting any firm answers. So we must of necessity return to our question: How far are these things real events and how far are they theological proclamations? They could of course be both, but the real question is how far the historical is subservient to the theological so that the theological determines and controls what is presented as history. Many things we can let go quite easily. Some, like angels, are quite simply forms of expression of the first century and are merely what a man of those times would have expected to see. They are merely his description of contact with the divine. The same may be said of dreams and visions; they just would not enter into our description of events. The stories around John the Baptist are there simply to link him with Jesus and are taken almost in their entirety out of the Old Testament. The speeches and the songs express such a unified theological outlook that they are seen to come from one source, either from one stream of tradition or, in our opinion more likely, from the pen of Luke himself. They are perfect expressions of his own theological ideas and hardly express impromptu utterances however inspired.

But what about more important things like the census, the journey to Bethlehem, the lying in the manger, and the visit of the shepherds?

How far are these based on strong tradition? Can we even go back as far
as Mary herself?

Attractive in many ways though this theory is, it nevertheless in the
last resort seems to go further than the evidence itself will actually allow.
Though Luke and John suggest that Mary was numbered among the
followers of Jesus during his ministry, it is otherwise in Mark 3.21, 35
where Mary stands in some form of contrast, even of opposition to him.
In verse 21 she seems to be among those who find Jesus incomprehen-
sible. Luke, however, makes Mary a believer during the life-time of
Jesus and a member of the post-resurrection earliest Christian community. Those verses which represent her as pondering upon the events
surrounding the birth of Jesus may then be included, not to record how
he received these items, but to link the whole career of Jesus and to make
Mary the representative of the true in Israel who have understood the
significance of Jesus and so have responded to God's action in him.

That this is the more likely explanation of these references is suggested, not only by our understanding of the Annunciation scene as a
response to a tradition rather than as the reporting of the historical basis
of that tradition, but also by the difficulties surrounding a possible universal census around 6 BC, by the not easily explained reference to
Quirinius for this period, by the scanty and unco-ordinated references
to the Roman census requirements which are said to have led Mary and
Joseph to Bethlehem, and by the confusion in Luke's reporting of the
visit to the Temple where the Jewish ceremonies are clearly ill understood. All this does not suggest the presence of a strong eye-witness
tradition. At best it can suggest a possible eye-witness link which has
become garbled in the hearing and overlaid with details which are
included wholly for their theological significance.

And so we have to come back to the point where we allow that we just
do not know what history there is in these stories other than response to
a tradition that Jesus was born at Bethlehem of a virgin betrothed to a
son of David in the days of Herod the king. However, such is the historically loose way that even these 'facts' are handled by our two evangelists that our acceptance of them as 'hard' history must in the end depend
upon the strength of the tradition underlying the New Testament as a
whole rather than upon the actual accounts of Matthew and Luke.

What is common to both sets of infancy narratives is the belief that
God's final, complete saving activity was present in Jesus of Nazareth,
and that his birth summed up and prefigured what was God's total act
in him. Luke's song of the angels points forward to the Ascension just as

Matthew's worship of the wise men is linked to the risen Christ's commission of the universal witness. Here is to be found the real significance of the infancy narratives. They are proclamations of faith rather than the actual grounds for coming to that faith. As proclamations, rather than reports, they have in mind the whole career of Jesus rather than just one part – even though it be that actual earthly beginnings – of that life. They reflect responses to his whole career rather than to his birth alone, and they describe a Christian rather than a pre-Christian faith.

For this reason the infancy narratives are often described as midrash. This literary type was widespread among the Jews and was basically a free exposition of scripture in the form of a commentary, additional incidents, and sometimes a rewriting of the original in order to make it bear more immediately and significantly upon the present. It employed a skilful use of the imagination in an effort to draw out the significance of the original proclamation and to make it relevant for a later age. Through it scripture became intelligible to later generations and met them with an ever new statement and demand.

In the infancy narratives, the Old Testament becomes the tool rather than the ultimate object of inspired reflection. Yet, in spite of this particular difference in the subject of the Jewish and Christian midrashim, in other ways there is a very close unity of outlook between them. By using Old Testament prefigurations, by building stories around them and by presenting Jesus as one with the Old Testament figures and as the fulfilment of the old covenant's hopes, they were able to draw out the significance of the birth of Jesus as they saw it and as it summed up for them that complete saving presence of God which had embraced them in his whole event.

The infancy narratives themselves suggest that this is the way that they should be approached, for they themselves do not allow us to use them in any more precise, any more clearly defined, manner. They come before us as witnesses to faith in the exalted Jesus of Nazareth, inviting us to share in their response of faith, rather than as statements of events which are to be accepted as themselves the basis for faith. If, for instance, we are able to share in their faith in the virgin birth of Jesus, it is because both Luke and Matthew witness to a tradition which we feel has historical truth behind it and which has been sustained by Christian tradition over the centuries, rather than because we think that either Matthew or Luke, or indeed both, present an historical account of what actually happened at a particular moment in time. Their ultimate value is to be found in their proclamation for

which the stories are the vehicles rather than in the facts of the stories
themselves.

The stories are in reality the products of faith rather than being in
themselves the literal basis for believing in what they proclaim. The
reason for belief remains firmly based in the whole event of the life,
death, and resurrection of Jesus and in the subsequent life of the believing community empowered by him. This is not to reduce the infancy
narratives, and it is certainly not to equate them with fiction. They are
proclamations of God's saving act in Jesus and, as that, are included in
God's revelation of himself as they themselves can be accepted as a
significant part of the whole saving event. We actually come to believe
with them rather than because of them, for they play the same part in
their gospels that John's prologue plays in his. They are the statement
which the ensuing gospel then as a whole justifies, spells-out, and
unfolds.

There is all the difference in the world between theological proclamation and story, for the former informs, challenges, and proclaims in a
way that is completely impossible to the latter. So, our first task as
preachers is to move them from the realm of story into that of theological
proclamation – into a kerygma which can both challenge and raise the
assumptions of those who hear them. And perhaps the first way by
which we do this is by being absolutely open – even by being ruthlessly
honest – about our understanding of their relation to 'hard' history. We
need to say that the historical content in them is actually beyond our
ability to establish, that this anyway is not the point which the evangelists wanted to get across when they wrote their narratives, and that we
must look at them as proclamations of the evangelists' deeply held
beliefs about Jesus which they conveyed in the form of historical writing
but which in accordance with the outlook of their age and of the traditions which they used did in fact contain only a minimum of hard facts.
We preach them as belief, as the witness of the early church to their
knowledge that in Jesus they had been grasped by God himself. The real
historical witness of these narratives is to be found, not in some series of
events happening in (say) the years around 6 BC but in the belief of the
evangelists and their communities in the years around (say) AD 85 and
in the fact that something happened in the life, death, and believed-in
resurrection of Jesus of Nazareth around (say) the years AD 25–30 to call
such beliefs into being.

Nevertheless, we still have to face the fact that our understanding of
them as kerygma – as proclamation, as testimony – does not necessarily

mean that they still have something to say to us. We might recognize the skill of their narrators and admit to the value of their proclamation for their contemporaries but that does not necessarily mark them out as having a significant contribution to make to our own attempts to understand and to proclaim God's action in Jesus. So, how are we to preach them? Can we use their themes legitimately now or do we have to leave them aside to make our proclamation of Jesus in our own way? How can they give content to our proclamation?[5]

Matthew's narrative will cause us the greater difficulty for, apart from the story of the wise men, it is centred almost entirely upon justifying a belief in Jesus to those who accepted the evangelists' own understanding of the validity of the Old Testament and of Old Testament patterns. Hence the artificial genealogy, the use of proof texts, and the obvious links between Joseph the father of Jesus and Joseph the enabler of the great Old Testament saving event, the Exodus. The Old Testament is being used here creatively, but also as a means of backing-up, of legitimizing, belief in Jesus. It is used in fact to soften the scandal of Jesus, to bring him into line, to justify belief in him. He is of the line of David, he is the climax of Israel's history, he is following the pattern laid down by the saviours of old. The scandal of his earthly career is thereby reduced. Faith in him is validated, it is saved from the total offence which the cross makes it.

And here is Matthew's weakness. Here is the point at which we enter into dialogue with the evangelist and let even his limitations be a means of encouraging our fuller surrender. We shall accept his proclamation that Jesus is Emmanuel, that in him God is with us as he abides in his church ('Lo, I am with you always'). We shall admire the commitment of his message, but we shall at the same time see how the message itself transcends and breaks free from all the attempts to make it more acceptable, more digestible, more open to conformity with expectations and hopes. Such attempts hold down its power and stop faith from being real surrender. Matthew had not yet learned the full extent of the stumbling-block presented by the cross.

The story of the wise men on the other hand, is much more easily entered into. Here is to be found creative rather than literal use of the Old Testament which is made to produce a word-picture which has appealed both to the imagination and to the Spirit-led insights of later ages.

The wise men represent those of all ages who have searched for truth, for meaning, for significance in life – all who have not kept their eyes within the limits of the material but who have engaged upon the search for reality – all who have been open to awe, to wonder, to the God of a thousand names and actions. They represent all who watch and wait, all who are prepared to set out on the journey in search of true being. That journey, says Matthew, leads them to a place they do not expect and to a person who is other than they visualized him. It leads them not to a palace but to a house, not to one who has the obvious trappings of monarchy, but to a babe in a peasant woman's arms. It leads them – if they will follow it – to Jesus who is proclaimed as the answer to their searchings, the fulfilment of their hopes. But the discovery at the end of their journey represents nevertheless a judgment on their expectations. Jewry in the person of Herod rejects him for he threatens its stability, he upends its expectations, he shatters its privileged status. So Herod will seek him out only to destroy him. But though he may kill, he can never destroy, for Jesus really is God's action, and God's will, though thwarted, will just not be brought to nothing.

And the wise men? They offer their gifts. The offering must in itself have been an act of faith for Jesus did not fulfil their expectations. They had looked for a royal child and they found only a workman's son. For the Son is father to the man, and the man himself was a carpenter, hung upon a cross, risen yes, but in such a way as to be unobvious, to remain rejected and scorned. But the faith of the wise men triumphs and they offer their gifts. That Matthew saw in the wise men the offering of the first-fruits of the Gentiles is clear. Less clear is the actual significance he found in that offering. Do the gifts represent a giving or a giving up? Are the wise men offering the best of their lives, their work, their arts, their possessions, or are they surrendering their unworthy illicit crafts of darkness before the light of truth and grace? How much judgment is involved when they acknowledge Jesus? Evaluations vary. It is true that earlier exponents of the wise men's art often appear in the Old Testament in a hostile guise. If Joseph's adversaries are impotent, Moses' opponents are blameworthy. Later members of the club earn the condemnation of the worshippers of the true God. Yet Matthew's wise men have no trace of evil or deceit about them. Their acknowledgment of Jesus is not said to be unworthy: their gifts are not spurned. They are open to the divine communications and they follow the star while Jewry malevolently stays at home. Part astrologers, part inheritors of the wisdom of the ages, part statesmen, part intellectuals, they are open to the signs of the times, and those signs lead them to Jesus. Matthew most probably put them forward for our approval, and their appeal to the ages is unlikely to be out of sympathy with his original intention. Matthew saw them, in the light of the Gentiles in his church, as those who were open to receive the kingdom, and the final command of the glorified Christ in his gospel is one that proclaims acceptance rather than judgment, fulfilment rather than condemnation.

And it is as this that we preach Matthew's story today. Jesus is Emmanuel – God with us – for all men. He meets us with a message of acceptance, with a promise of fulfilment. But to find him demands a search and, above all, a willingness to enter upon a search. It means lifting one's eyes from the ground, ceasing to be hemmed in by the material. It means responding to a measure of divine discontent. It means a journey and the consequent willingness to go forward in a trust which is prepared to let go of the familiar, to abandon what had come to be looked upon as security. And when we find Jesus? It results in a total challenge, a complete overturning of our expectations, for Jesus is almost always found to give the answer 'no' when we expect and want 'yes', and to say 'yes' when we expect 'no'. We want a child in a palace and we have to be prepared to accept a working man on a cross. And the offering of our gifts means both a giving and a giving up, for his acceptance of us inevitably means a judgment upon us. In preaching on the wise men we are preaching on nothing less than Jesus crucified and risen, on him as God's answer to the needs of the world.

And so it is with Luke's infancy narratives which have always had a wide appeal but which as we have seen can all too easily be evacuated of their true message. Two things have to be brought out in our preaching upon these – Luke's confident proclamation that Jesus really is God's total answer to the hopes of mankind, the complete fulfilment of earlier promises, but also, and nevertheless, the hidden nature, the ambiguity that is part and parcel of that answer. Luke's proclamation of faith is a summons to faith, to commitment to him who though hidden really is both Lord and Christ. His first two chapters serve as an unfolding of the proclamation given in Peter's Pentecost sermon: 'Let all the house of Israel know assuredly that God has made him both Lord and Christ, this Jesus whom you crucified.'

Luke's Old Testament imagery – his unfolding of these early narratives in Old Testament terms and with the help of Old Testament patterns – are at once a statement of his faith and of his commitment to Jesus. They are a declaration that in him there is to be found, in the witness of the angelic hymn: 'Glory to God in the highest and on earth peace to those in whom God's pleasure dwells.' God's salvation really has drawn near, and the career of Jesus – his life, death, resurrection and ascension, and the universal witness of the new community under the inspiration of the Holy Spirit – can be interpreted as nothing less than this. His two volumes will unpack and justify his faith which the infancy narratives proclaim so magnificently.

Jesus therefore is the climax of all God's action in the old Israel. Her history comes to a climax in him: her saving figures find their fulfilment in him. Through him, God has 'visited and redeemed his people', he has given 'light to those who sit in darkness and in the shadow of death' and he has guided 'our feet into the way of peace'. And so in the concluding act of the infancy narratives, the aged Simeon and the prophetess Anna, representatives of the piety of Israel and of those who looked for her renewal, acknowledge Jesus as the 'glory to thy people Israel.' We shall miss Luke's message, we shall fail to capture his sense of fulfilment, of joy, of liberation in Jesus unless we do justice to this Old Testament dimension of these stories, for Luke was, though a Gentile, a man of the book, one, probably a god-fearer, who had found his life in Jesus by way of his earlier entry into the promises of the Old Testament. In the Old Testament and its message – in some sort of relation to the Jewish people – Luke had begun to find an answer to his own longings and hopes. In Jesus he had found those longings fulfilled. Jesus really was God's answer to the needs of mankind. In him God had acted fully and completely. His Old Testament imagery therefore expresses both the reality of his expectations and of his searchings, and also the magnitude of his proclamation. It enabled him to put his all into his message, for he could imagine no greater way of expressing his convictions.

It is true of course that we cannot get the same commitment out of the Old Testament's imagery. We cannot share Luke's pilgrimage to Jesus by way of a partial freedom found in the faith of Israel, so we cannot quite share the wonder and excitement that comes across in Luke's writings. But we can appreciate something of their atmosphere as we sum up at Christmas time the significance of Jesus as we have found him within the corporate experience of the Christian community. For Luke's narratives set the individual's faith firmly within the context of that of the people of God. Here is no individual's proclamation conveyed in isolation, but the message of one who has found God's salvation in Jesus expressed and conveyed in the making of a nation, of a people 'created for his own name'. At Christmas we who are preachers are given a proclamation that is real as it is conveyed through our own sense of having been grasped by God as we have been incorporated into his community, the church.

Luke's community has a world-wide dimension. Jesus is born at just the time when the whole world is on the move. 'And all went to be enrolled, each to his own city.' The world was in turmoil and in expectation; it was in a state both of anxiety and of unrest, of hope and of optimism. All these emotions are present at an enrolling – almost those that mark the birth of a nation. It was at just this juncture that Jesus was born. 'In those days there went out a decree from Caesar Augustus that all the world should be enrolled.' Luke already points to the universal significance of Jesus. The world is not closed to the power of God for, unwittingly, the great Roman empire contributes to his purposes since its decree brings Joseph and Mary to Bethlehem and so enables Jesus to be born in David's city. Uncomprehending of Christianity the Roman state of Luke's day may have been, but Luke's God can still use it – it is not outside his influence – and use it he does to bring Jesus to Bethlehem just as later he will use it to bring the rejected one to his resurrection and the leading disciple, Paul, to Rome.

For Luke is ultimately a theologian of hope. This will be the next point in our proclamation of these narratives. He proclaims hope, not that hope which oozes 'peace on earth, goodwill towards men' in some starry-eyed sentimental exercise, but the ultimate hope based on belief in the God who stands behind Jesus and upon a realistic optimism about men who, whether they know it or not, are not totally divorced from God or completely apart from his influence. Jesus stands in some almost indefinable way for belief in a real link between God and man. His birth which, as an anticipation of his whole career, makes possible 'Glory to God in the highest', does so as man in this world is enabled to live within the influence of the kingdom. God's kingdom, established already in the heavens, enables and empowers the victory of man's highest aspirations here on earth. The Magnificat is a proclamation of this belief whilst in the Nunc Dimittis Jesus is seen not only as Israel's glory but also as the light to all nations. In him Isaianic hopes are realized: 'And the glory of the Lord shall be revealed and all flesh shall see it together, for the mouth of the Lord has spoken' (Isa. 40.5).

But Luke's hope is also realistic. Jesus remains the hidden Messiah – the Lord whose full glory is seen only in heaven. Here is the challenge of Luke – that we should accept that hiddenness, that we should come to terms with the obscurity of the one whom we confess as Lord so that we will not be offended by the rejection of him by the vast majority of our contemporaries. For Luke's two volumes do not tell a story of over-whelming success. Though the message goes from Jerusalem to Rome, it does so only by way of Jewish rejection and of Gentile indifference, by way of one who reaches Rome as a prisoner. Luke's story which is so often presented as a first chapter in an ongoing, triumphant, barnstorm-ing mission is not really that at all. It is a story of what faith sees as universal witness to the truth, but it is a story which has to be seen in its faith-dimension for, without that, it could easily be presented as near-failure. Luke was far less naive on this point than some of his modern interpreters and the universal witness was no more obviously an un-inhibited witness to the unclouded power of God than was the earthly life of the Lord who set it first in motion.

And so Luke's infancy narratives emphasize the hiddenness, the obscurity, even the seeming ambivalence of the saving event. 'There was no place for them in the inn.' Though Luke writes more in sorrow than in anger, he nevertheless points to the tragedy inherent in this situation. Israel rejects her Lord, makes no room for him. But if in the first instance Bethlehem represents his own people, it stands also for all religious life which so easily makes God in its own image and so fails to recognize him when he comes. But Bethlehem is now linked to the whole world on the move and which is too busy seeking its own salvation to notice the one who can bring it.

So Jesus is born not in the inn but outside it. Here, indeed, is hidden-ness at its most intense. Earlier, the prophet Jeremiah had spoken of God's obscure presence in Israel: 'O thou hope of Israel, its saviour in time of trouble, why shouldest thou be like a stranger in the land, like a wayfarer who turns aside to tarry for a night?' (Jer. 14.8). The Septua-gint, Luke's Bible, reads, 'Like a wayfarer turning aside into a lodging'. It uses the same word as Luke uses here and which is usually translated 'inn'. Jeremiah's hidden God was like one who lodged merely tem-porarily in an inn, and he longed for him to be more open, more com-pelling, more vindicating, more obviously present. Luke's Lord could not even find a lodging. He was laid in a manger, and, again, Old Testa-ment prophecy provided the background. Isaiah of old had chided Israel for her failure to acknowledge her Lord: 'The ox knows its owner, and the ass its master's crib; but Israel does not know, my people does not understand' (Isa. 1.2–3). Jesus is unacknowledged except by his family – his people, the people of God – and by the shepherds who represent the outcast and the despised, the rejected and the irreligious, who were to play such a leading part in Jesus' ministry as Luke records it. This comment on the shepherds says all that needs to be said: 'We miss the meaning of the shepherds if we think of them only as nice, old gentlemen with pious, weather-beaten faces and white beards. . . . Luke knew that shepherds were <u>outsiders in Israel</u>. Pious people looked on them askance. Because of their job, they couldn't keep the whole of the Law; the sabbath rest, the detailed ritual, the washing of hands and places and all the other rubrics of purification. They used, sometimes of necessity, to pasture their sheep in foreign territory as a result of which trespassing they were considered "unclean". Like the tax-collectors, the shepherds by profession were <u>sinners and excommunicate</u>. Luke's message is: It is for people of this sort that Jesus has come.'[6] There is irony, as well as both sadness and joy, in Luke's story, and this adds to that hidden glory which he saw surrounding the whole life of the Lord.

The sign to the shepherds is a 'babe wrapped in swaddling clothes and lying in a manger.' In its own way, this comes close to the sign of Jesus to Luke's readers – and it can be close to the sign that is put before us. Jesus is the rejected one, the hidden one, but he, within that situation of rejection, is also the acknowledged one. Mary wraps him in swaddling clothes. Ezekiel had earlier drawn a picture of Israel's beginnings when no one had cared for her. 'And as for your birth, on the day you were born, your navel string was not cut, nor were you washed with water to cleanse you, nor rubbed with salt, nor swathed with bands' (Ezek. 16.4). Jesus was laid in a manger, unacknowledged by the world at large, but he was not uncared for, unrecognized. The swathing bands are a mark of caring, a sign of recognition by his mother, Mary, who in Luke's narrative seems to represent the true people of God, 'the handmaid of the Lord,' the faithful ones who watched, wondered, believed, and waited. The angel announces him, not only as Christ, but also as Lord, and this as Luke's favourite designation for Jesus, represents the response of faith, a declaration of universal status, one wider than that of Messiah. Jesus is Lord of all who believe in him, and, because he is their Lord, they can declare his enthronement at God's right hand. The faith response of the individual – cemented within the response of the believing community – is ultimately the reason for faith in his universal Lordship. It is both its source and its guarantee.

And it is as those within the believing community who recognize Jesus as Lord that we proclaim him through the infancy narratives. They can be used by us to become the supreme expression of our faith in him and as the supreme challenge to us to deepen that faith as we understand more about God's action through him. They can become our proclamation of Jesus, crucified, risen and ascended, and they can help us to acknowledge his Lordship – real though hidden – as we respond to it within the community of his church.

The Resurrection Narratives

Belief in the resurrection of Jesus is at the heart of the New Testament proclamation; indeed, without it, there would have been no message at all to proclaim. On this point Paul speaks on behalf of all the New Testament witnesses when he writes to the church at Corinth that 'if Christ has not been raised, then our preaching is in vain and your faith is in vain' (I Cor. 15.14). The angelic proclamation, 'He has risen, he is not here' remains the grounds of the New Testament's faith and the justification for its hope. Now as then it demands our assent to this as the very core of its announcement and as the most fundamental article of its belief. 'Blessed be the God and Father of our Lord Jesus Christ! By his great mercy we have been born anew to a living hope through the resurrection of Jesus Christ from the dead' (I Peter 1.3). It is not too much to say that the whole of the New Testament represents the unpacking of this proclamation.

But of what exactly should belief in the resurrection of Jesus consist? What does the New Testament put before us for our assent when it makes its proclamation? It expresses belief in both a factual event and also the significance of that event. Our difficulty is to know how these two are interrelated in the gospel narratives and to determine the influence of each upon the individual stories.

For most people, talk about the resurrection of Jesus suggests talk about the resuscitation of his body. 'The resurrection' expresses ideas and expectations which are of the same order as those found in a verse inscribed on an eighteenth century tombstone:

> Here I lie sleeping in the dust,
> > Until the rising of the just.
> Until our Saviour he shall say,
> > 'Arise, ye dead, and come away'.

For them, Jesus' resurrection can be nothing other than the resuscitation of the dead body, its removal from the tomb, its transformation to enable its appearance in various modes to the disciples, and its glorification to accomplish its entry into the heavenly sphere. This is what the gospels seem to be suggesting and this form of belief is what it is generally assumed they require.

For some, though, this gives rise to a problem which occasions real doubt and disbelief and this is not just a question of a lack of faith or of some arrogance before a divine act. It is rather a genuine perplexity brought about primarily by the sheer difficulties and inconsistencies of the biblical narratives when these are taken outside the community of faith and subjected to the cold light of enquiry and critical, if not sceptical, scrutiny. I well remember the perplexity of one headmaster who felt duty-bound to read some of the resurrection stories in assembly at the beginning of the Easter term, but who confessed to me that he just did not know what to make of them for himself and was almost afraid to think what impression they made upon the boys.

Yet the narratives do make sense when they are read and expounded within the community of faith, and inconsistencies take on the nature of insignificance as their message strikes responsive chords in the understanding of the believing congregation. It is not that the historical problems disappear. I remain just as aware of them when I am a part of the eucharistic congregation as I am when I hear them at school assembly. It is simply that, within that context, they, for the time, become irrelevant. The narratives' point of contact with me occurs, not at some event that happened nearly two thousand years ago, but in the present. They unfold, explain, judge, and deepen my awareness of the Christ who is encountered in the here and now. The resurrection becomes, not an event of the past, but one of the present. Easter is now, and they speak of a past event only in the light of the present experience, for it is the present encounter with the risen Christ which gives reality to the proclamation of past experiences. These stories live – they ring true – only as their experience unites me to the experiences of those who told them, not in the way that my experience and theirs must be identical, but in the sense that my experience must have a real point of contact with theirs. In a word, we are all part of that same community which has been brought into being by the whole event centred in Jesus Christ. As we hear the resurrection narratives within the life of the community of faith, we approach them with presuppositions which are of the same family-likeness as those which were held by the early church as it told them and by the evangelists as they wrote them down.

And it is these presuppositions which determine, not only what the first century caused to be written down and the form in which they expressed it, but also the way in which we hear their proclamation now.

What we hear – from our real vantage point within the community of faith – is wholly other than that which comes across to those outside. Whilst we continue to be very grateful for our vantage point, this should not shroud us from their problems or make us insensitive to the difficulties that the resurrection stories present to them. The preacher must aim, not only to deepen the faith of the believer, but also to make him sensitive to the alleged faithlessness of the unbeliever. These two parts of his task are not unconnected, for he must seek continually to expose the real nature of faith and to deepen its reality in the lives of his hearers.

But all this means that we are already in some way entering into the minds of the evangelists and accepting them as proclaimers of a present reality rather than just as historians of something that happened long ago. For us as for them, the present is already exerting a controlling influence over the receiving and telling of past events. Take away the present and the narratives' accounts of the past become something of a dead exercise, open to the charges both of inconsistency and of inconsequential reporting. They become, inevitably, an unsatisfactory record for, viewed in such a light, they fail to answer seemingly legitimate questions in anything like a satisfactory way. And this, of course, should cause us no surprise for, as we have been arguing throughout these chapters, the gospel narratives are to be seen in the first place as evidence for the faith of the early church as it tried to express its response to Jesus of Nazareth whom it now knew as its living Lord. They witness to their beliefs, and they understand Jesus in the light of these. For us, belief in the resurrection of Jesus depends primarily upon a sharing in the faith of the early church and only secondarily upon the actual historical details in the stories they told. The stories point us beyond themselves to the faith of those who told them. The narratives are to be viewed as expressions of this, and their truth is found, not in their factual correctness, but in the reality of the faith they articulate.

Problems for the man of faith come primarily in the story of the empty tomb because, faced with this, he has either to acknowledge consciously just how much of an element of interpretation he is actually allowing to the biblical writers, or because here he is faced with what is to him historical scepticism both within and without the believing community. 'Was the tomb empty?' becomes inevitably the point at which the crunch comes and lines of battle are drawn.

It is undoubtedly true that suggestions that the body of Jesus may not have risen physically from the tomb cause considerable hurt to a large number of Christians, since they seem to deny belief in the resurrection itself. Some recent discussions have even maintained that if Jesus' bones could be discovered undisturbed in Palestine, then confidence in the Christian proclamation would be destroyed and faith in Jesus would be wholly undermined. More widely, when Professor Geoffrey Lampe, in a television programme on Easter Day 1965, stated that he regarded the story of the empty tomb as a profoundly significant myth rather than as literal history, he provoked a great deal of correspondence which was both highly critical of, and deeply distressed by his remark.[7]

The problem seems really to divide itself into two parts, namely, 'Does disbelief in, or doubt about, the empty tomb mean disbelief in or doubt about the actual resurrection of Jesus?' and 'Does disbelief in, or doubt about, the empty tomb mean that there is no longer any objective proof of the resurrection and therefore of the beliefs of Christianity as such?' It seems important that these two aspects of the problem should not be confused.

Does belief in the resurrection of Jesus require belief in the actual physical resurrection of his body? This is undoubtedly what the New Testament as a whole believed even though there remains some doubt as to whether Paul (who in I Cor. 15.4–8 is our earliest witness), himself thought of an empty tomb. There he writes that Jesus 'died for our sins in accordance with the scriptures, that he was buried, that he was raised on the third day in accordance with the scriptures, and that he appeared to Cephas, then to the Twelve. Then he appeared to more than five hundred brethren at once, most of whom are still alive, though some have fallen asleep. Then he appeared to James, then to all the apostles. Last of all, as to one untimely born, he appeared also to me.' On the whole, it seems likely that Paul is thinking here of the empty tomb – his use of 'buried' and 'was raised on the third day' certainly seems to suggest that – though, since 'buried' is there simply to underline the reality of the death of Jesus, the reference to his being raised 'on the third day' may be included merely to point to the reality of the risen life. At any rate, the empty tomb is not seen as the significant event, which is rather the appearances to the witnesses, and belief in the resurrection is inferred from them. For Paul, the empty tomb has little meaning in itself but is primarily part of the interpretation of the significance of the appearances. Given the apocalyptic outlook of Paul and of the New Testament writers generally, they could have thought of the overcoming of death and of the continuing reality of the life of Jesus only in terms of the resurrection of the physical body and so of its leaving the tomb. Just as eighteenth-century Christians knew of no complete overcoming of

death and of the reality of a future life without the physical resuscitation
and transformation, so the New Testament writers could only envisage
Jesus' vindication in terms of physical categories. The framework of
their thought demanded this.

Yet their actual experience did not. Paul included his own conversion
experience as one with, and as the last of, the resurrection appearances
of Jesus to his followers. Elsewhere, he can say, 'Have not I seen Jesus
our Lord?' (I Cor. 9.1) and can proclaim how God 'was pleased to
reveal his son to me' (Gal. 1.16). In I Cor. 15 he does not suggest that
Jesus' appearance to him was in any way different from those to the
earlier witnesses of the resurrection. Yet the descriptions of that appearance in Acts 9, 22, and 26 suggest a visionary rather than a physical
manifestation, and this somewhat tenuous character of the appearances
is confirmed by many of the gospel narratives themselves.

All this, together with the general understanding of the gospels which
allows that they sometimes did write up traditions and even create narratives which embodied belief in a historical and factual form, suggests
that the appearances of Jesus were not actual physical manifestations of
his presence, but that the impact of his appearances has been concentrated in a series of stories which have been further embellished by the
early church's understanding of the real presence of Jesus in their midst.
Many of the 'facts' could well have been created: the reality behind the
facts, we believe, could not.

The reality is found in the belief that Jesus was seen by the disciples
after his death, that something had happened to convince them that he
was alive and to cause them to believe that death had not had the last
word with him. Moreover, this event was seen to be an act of God himself, a vindication of his commitment to Jesus and a declaration that in
him God had vanquished evil and established the ultimacy of those
concerns and certainties which Jesus had demonstrated and proclaimed.
The manner of this encounter can perhaps best be described as an
objective vision – as a visionary appearance which did in fact impinge
upon the understanding and the emotions of those who were gripped by
it. At Easter something happened to grasp the disciples, to convince
them that Jesus was alive and to demonstrate the ultimacy of Jesus and
the reality of the God who stands behind him. For the New Testament
as a whole the resurrection is the ultimate basis of the Christian's confidence; it represents the beginnings of the final victory over evil and
becomes the guarantee and pledge of the vindication of goodness and
truth.

The resurrection then established the Lordship of Jesus and proclaims its open revelation in the future. It represents nothing less than a decisive act of God which ensures its completion in some future act when the Lordship of Christ will become a reality which all will see. The resurrection has vindicated Jesus and has enabled Christians already to share in its triumph even if its fullness for them is reserved for the future. At the resurrection God acted to bring about this new realization and, in doing so, he gave an assurance of purpose, hope, and of a future to those who are given life through him. It is the resurrection of Jesus which in the last resort enables us to believe in a God whose love will never let us down.[8]

This would seem to be a fair and adequate translation of what the New Testament writers understood by the resurrection of Jesus, of the meaning behind their descriptions, and of the significance they ascribed to the actual event. It accepts that they were writing in imagery derived from the first century and that their outlook towards historical reporting was of an age other than our own. But it is true to the convictions of the New Testament writers and in no way belittles or undercuts their proclamation.

But does it do justice to the gospels' assertions of the empty tomb? What element does that belief supply to the resurrection faith and has our restatement done justice to that? If I understand them aright, writers who stress the significance of the empty tomb are maintaining that belief in it gives witness to the fact that God has begun actually to act in the physical world as we know it, that he can already bring about transformation within it, and that he will eventually effect its fulfilment and make it completely open to his will. The physical resurrection of Jesus, witnessed to by the empty tomb, is a mark of world affirmation, a sign of God's intervention even now in the physical world, and a guarantee of his future redemption of it.[9]

Yet it is doubtful if this is really what the New Testament intends to assert. The New Testament itself sees the resurrection as the beginning and pledge of God's final sovereignty; it views it as the beginning of the new age; the pledge and guarantee of the end. It anticipated the Parousia. But that event expressed belief in a tension between this world and God's love, for it maintained that this world could never of itself be wholly open to that love. So the New Testament did not see the resurrection as the point at which this world as it is was grasped by God. God's action remains within the world, hidden in its main effects, open only to the eyes of faith. The resurrection vindicated Jesus, but it did so, not demonstrably and irrefutably, but in a way to be perceived by faith and accepted through experience.

The understanding of the resurrection that we have been outlining does not allow for that element of proof, of assuredness, which a literal acceptance of the narratives would seem to make possible. Perhaps this, ultimately, is what distresses people most and causes most resentment. How often do we hear critics of this approach quote, as an accusation, Mary's cry of anguish, 'They have taken away my Lord and I know not where they have laid him'? No radical critic of the gospels can be insensitive to the hurt in this cry or unmindful of his responsibility in causing it. Yet his concern for truth and his responsibility to what he understands to be the nature of Christian commitment will not let him be silent, even though he himself enters upon his course with no little trembling. What he sees as the demands of his biblical understanding, what is suggested by these as the true nature of faith, and what is thrust upon him by his contemporary experience, unite to suggest that God's vindication of Jesus at the resurrection was not a clear irrefutable act, demonstrably true, and of the nature of an open manifestation of his power, but was concealed and visible only to the eyes of faith.

To seek in the story of the empty tomb a demonstrable ground for faith is to deny the nature of faith itself and is ultimately to reduce the gospel. For the gospels themselves do not see the empty tomb as an open demonstration of the resurrection of Jesus. Only the beloved disciple in the Fourth Gospel accepts it as such, and his faith is pictured as extraordinary and clearly going beyond normal expectations. Elsewhere, the event has to be interpreted and, in Mark at any rate, it remains totally ambiguous. The way in which literal acceptance of the empty tomb has been variously explained so that belief in the resurrection might continue to be denied reminds us of this ambiguity. Always the empty tomb falls short of actual demonstration of Jesus' resurrection, and to seek to hold on to it as an event which does just that seems to be making it into a false resting place for faith which is then reduced to a level of proof or to a seeming certainty which rests upon something other than its really true basis which can only be a personal relationship with the living Lord. We would be asking for something as demonstrable as the descent from the pinnacle of the temple which the devil required or as the coming down from the cross which the false priests demanded.

That Easter Day was God's vindication of Jesus, that it represented the actual, divine reversal of evil's power, rampant on Good Friday, and that it gave a foretaste of the ultimate and complete victory of love is, as we have seen, a fundamental part of the New Testament's testimony. Belief in the resurrection of the Christ proclaims that the act of God really did take place even though its demonstration is available only to those who will enter upon the way of faith. Loyalty to the New Testament proclamation would appear to require assent to some such act, and its actual likelihood in fact is enhanced by the need to explain the rise of the resurrection faith amongst the disciples of Jesus.

For these reasons therefore we hesitate to follow those who maintain a somewhat different approach to these narratives which, though having much in common with the position we have been describing, departs from it at one important point.[10] Those who propound this approach allow that there was, indeed, an Easter event, but they maintain that this is to be found in nothing other than the disciples' arrival at faith. They came to see that Jesus had a continuing significance for them, that his life and death still impinged upon them to bring them release, freedom, and oneness with God. They now found God only in and through him, and his reality for them was such that he was still their contemporary. They lived because of him, and so they could think of his living in them. The miracle of Easter was the rise of this faith. This enshrined the event which reversed Good Friday. Jesus now lived in the lives of those who believed in him, through his present impact upon them, and they expressed this by proclaiming his resurrection. The heart of this belief is that Jesus is alive *for us*, and just what element of *extra nos* is implied by this *pro nobis* it is impossible to say, for that is a question which goes beyond faith's ability to answer. The continuing, living reality is God, and he is experienced completely through Jesus.

In this view, the faith of the early church is itself responsible for the rise of belief in the resurrection of Jesus, whereas in the other views that we have been discussing, some more immediate act of God is believed to have given birth to the belief and so to have been ultimately responsible for the rise of faith. The question this new approach raises is whether it represents an adequate translation of the convictions which lie at the heart of the New Testament proclamation and whether it can offer a reasonable explanation for the actual historical rise of the Easter faith.

Can it account for the disciples' coming to faith in Jesus? Does it really do justice to the impact which, in the light of Good Friday, would seem to have been needed to bring this about? That Jesus himself made a deep impression on his disciples during the course of his ministry would seem undeniable – even though advocates of this view tend to minimize the significance of his life – but would it have been strong enough to withstand the seeming catastrophe of Good Friday? Did the disaster leave the disciples with enough convictions about Jesus to enable them to continue to have faith in him and to make the assertions which the New Testament records? Alternatively, could the real failure of the disciples to support Jesus in his hour of need actually have rebounded upon them to create in them a new awareness, a new decisiveness, and a new apprehension of the significance of Jesus? Could the heart of the change have been Peter's denial which so overwhelmed him that a new insight followed? Luke 22.31–32 could, after all, suggest something like such an estimate: 'Simon, Simon, behold Satan demanded to have you (all), that he might sift you (all) like wheat; but I prayed for you (yourself) that your (own) faith may not fail: and when you have turned again, strengthen your brethren.' If Jesus had foreseen and proclaimed his death, he certainly had not done so without giving some clear idea that he expected it to lead to his vindication. Some future act was certainly not totally unexpected, nor was it necessarily unlooked for. Upon reflection, and after the immediate physical danger had passed, Jesus' death could have been seen as the harbinger of the victory that he had anticipated.

Such reasonings on the part of the disciples cannot be completely ruled out and they may have caused the rise of the Easter faith. Equally, however, such a view cannot be dismissed as wholly subjective – 'the subjective vision hypothesis' – for it does not rule out the action of God himself upon the hearts and minds of those who embraced it. Nevertheless, by itself it still seems somewhat inadequate to explain either the rise of faith or to do justice to the characteristic New Testament proclamation.

The New Testament understanding puts forward for belief the proclamation of a real and paradigmatic act of God which vindicated Jesus and makes faith in him a pledge of our own future. How far the ideas of vindication and guarantee are to be viewed with suspicion as being Judaistic in outlook and unbaptized into that new understanding of God demanded by the cross of Christ is hard to say.[11] Plainly though we must allow that different views are possible on this point though we ourselves would find this last position less than completely satisfactory.

Whatever view we hold of the empty tomb however, we shall not base our proclamation on that but upon the faith of the early church expressed in its conviction that Jesus was alive and that he had made himself known to them. This is our Easter faith and it links our experience to theirs. The Prayer Book gospel for Easter Day was one of the less happy choices of that book. By reading only John's account of the finding of the empty tomb, it left the real message of Easter unproclaimed. Of itself, though open-ended, it was incomplete, and it inevitably fell flat. Having aroused the congregation's expectations, it failed completely to satisfy them. The new Anglican lectionary now extends the reading to include the story of Mary's desolation, of Jesus' appearing to her, of his proclamation of his exaltation, and concludes with Mary's exuberant witness to the disciples, 'I have seen the Lord'. This places the emphasis where the gospels themselves place it, and their narratives are attempts to unpack the truth of this witness as they unfold its continuing reality and significance for the life of the believing community.

This is in fact what we aim to do for our congregations – to base their understanding of the resurrection narratives upon their present experience of the risen Jesus in their midst, and in turn to expand their present encounter with him so that they deepen their commitment to him.

The individual stories are proclamations of the faith of the early community as they experienced his presence. Our aim therefore is to link their faith to the faith of our congregations. So the Emmaus story becomes primarily a story of our encounter with Jesus both in the scriptures and, supremely, in the eucharist. He is known to us in the breaking of the bread. The same is true of John's epilogue where Jesus meets his disciples in a meal which has clear eucharistic overtones and where his presence is experienced away from Jerusalem, the home of the extraordinary, and back in Galilee, the place of ordinary toil and of daily living. The twenty-first chapter of the gospel, though an obvious addition, is saved from the charge of anticlimax as it links the resurrection presence of Jesus to the hum-drum of ordinary life.

The resurrection narratives also see Christ's presence in the church as she shares in the response to his commission. If this is seen supremely in Luke's Ascension narrative, as it is given in Acts 1, it appears most obviously in Matthew's final commissioning scene and in John's Easter Day empowering of the disciples. Whilst Matthew presents the mission as undertaken in the power of the presence of the risen Jesus, Luke and John see it as empowered by the gift of the Holy Spirit.

If these episodes unfold the life of the believing community as it experiences the life of Jesus in it, other resurrection narratives point rather to the church's perplexity, and so try to come to terms with, and to justify the hidden nature of that presence. In our preaching, we will try to bring this out – just as the early church faced its problem of working out the nature of its presence in the world – and will try to bring its message to bear upon our present perplexities. The fact of Jesus' resurrection life is no more self-evident for us than it was for them. It was undoubtedly the hidden nature of Jesus' resurrection which caused Mark to give no resurrection narratives at all. He ends his gospel with the proclamation of the young man in the tomb which meets only with apprehension and wonder. The women are afraid, and although Mark may suggest awe and wonder before a divine event, more likely, I think, he brings out their sheer fear and perplexity. Their Lord though risen remains hidden from them. The angelic promise is one which looks to the future appearing of the Lord in glory. It is that hope which is going to strengthen them and bring them through fear to faith. Mark's gospel can meet our perplexity, our fearfulness, our longing. It can summon us to hope in the future and so bring us to understand the reality of Jesus' presence here and now.

Perplexity is found also in John's twentieth chapter which describes a progressive understanding and a journey to faith. From the first completely uncomprehending response of Mary Magdalene: 'They have taken away the lord out of the tomb, and we do not know where they have laid him', through the growing understanding of the empty tomb's significance, by way of the appearance first to the eleven and then to disbelieving Thomas, the response of faith gradually deepens until it proclaims the blessedness of those who, though not seeing, yet believe, and so seeks to include the gospel's readers in that gift. The whole narrative becomes an unfolding of the significance of the resurrection and of its reality in spite of its hiddenness. It is the church coming to terms with the need to be able to acknowledge the risen presence of Jesus in its midst. We in our times are called to go with the women of Mark's gospel from fear to faith, and to make that pilgrimage of deepening understanding which John's work unfolds so dramatically. Once again, the narratives bring us immediately into the present and exhibit their truth and their reality as the message they proclaim and the situation they unfold meet our situation and experience. Their power to inform is nothing unless they make their contact with us now. The way the individual stories are selected and handled by the different evangelists, and the way they are brought into the service of that evangelist's proclamation, shows that the existential appeal to present experience was uppermost in their author's minds.

It is the continuing experience of the believing community which these narratives seek to describe, and so to explain. Our aim in the pulpit will be to line ourselves up with them and so to enable their insights to unlock and to deepen our own. To concentrate on the past or to seek to uncover hard events within the narratives will only perplex. They tell of faith rather than facts. They point ultimately to one event only, and that is to the faith of the early church as it is based on the reality of Jesus' resurrection which brought it into being. We will not concentrate on the stories as though they described events of hard history, but will present them rather as witnessing to the faith of the early church and to its authenticity which is demonstrated as it finds points of contact with our own. We will go through the physical to unfold the reality that is to be found beyond it.

Our aim will be to unpack the evangelists' proclamations. Inevitably, however, as we do this we will be forced to take some stand upon the stories as events. Was the tomb empty? Did Jesus appear with a physical body however transformed? Was the ascension an event in time and of a particular place? Our congregations deserve an honest approach to these questions and, in the end, any attempt to skirt round them, to fudge the issue, or to leave gaps in our expositions will do much more harm than good. At some point in the Easter period, we have to make it clear that different Christians do hold different views on these questions, that, as we have seen, at least three different approaches can be taken to the stories of the empty tomb, and that none of these views can be declared illegitimate since they are all held by sincere Christian believers who are convinced that the path they follow is suggested, if not demanded, by the gospel narratives themselves.

This may be inconvenient, and it would no doubt be decried by some as being no 'gospel' at all since they would feel that good news requires a confident proclamation which both merits and demands assent. An uncertain trumpet does little for mankind they would say. Whilst this attitude is understandable, nevertheless the hard fact is that our gospel narratives do not allow such a measure of certainty that assent to one particular view of the empty tomb, say, is demanded by them, and all other views are therefore ruled out of court. Our gospels allow a diversity of belief here. I do not see how in all honesty that can be denied and I therefore do not see that we can do anything other than acknowledge this before our congregations.

Truth demands that our congregations should not be protected from this situation. Sadly, some will inevitably be hurt and we will go out of our way through our prayer, our sensitivity, and a recognition of our own very limited apprehension to minimize this. But the situation is such that we should not, even if it were possible, protect them completely from the hurt. We can only let them know that we share in that hurt and that it is a real sharing. Such must be the cross of the pastor.

But the hurt is diminished, and the living Christ is seen as an effective reality, when the narratives are preached as committed proclamations of faith, of conviction, of hope, and of trust. This all along will be our aim, and it will be achieved best as we preach these stories as witnesses of the living community which has found its life wholly in Jesus and which has therefore committed itself to him. In the end, it is this which carries conviction. It is the experience of the ages which enshrines the truth of the narratives; it is the life of the present community which will underpin our own faith which is then seen to rest, not upon the narratives themselves, but upon the faith of the people of God which they bring to expression.

And it is this which we will put before our congregations for their assent and so for their life. We will link them by word as well as by sacrament to those who have found their hope in Jesus crucified but alive. And in doing so, we will be asking our congregations to make that act of surrender, that act of dying to live, of letting go only to find, that Jesus demanded of Mary Magdalene. 'Do not hold me' was the risen Lord's call to her. She wanted to be able to embrace him, to discern him clearly, to identify him, to set bounds upon him, to objectify him. But she was told that this was something that she could not do. She had to let him go, for only so could he ascend to his Father. We too must cease to cling to the resurrected body of Jesus. We too have to let him go in this form, to rest our faith at another point – his Lordship over the community he has called into being. All four gospels point their readers into the future – that is of course into their own present. It is in the present that the risen Jesus must be found, and it is ultimately only the present which will give us that confidence which will enable us to say, 'The Lord is risen indeed!'

The Miracles

Preaching on the miracles is perhaps the most difficult task of all. The infancy narratives make their theological message clear and a preaching which is centred on this strikes responsive chords in many of our hearers. The resurrection narratives likewise take on a new context and a new dimension as they link up with and actually deepen our present experience of the risen Jesus in the midst of his people. The miracle stories however are more awkward and present us with even more complex problems for, whilst on the one hand they do not seem to tie up with reality as we understand and experience it, on the other hand to make them into something less than they appear to be seems to reduce the evangelists to the level of so many of their contemporaries who were little more than purveyors of naive tales and crude magic.

Two things seem to be necessary in our preaching on the miracles. In the first place, our proclamation must be a legitimate one. It must use them to proclaim a message which really is based upon the evangelists' own message. It must be worked out in genuine relationships with what they were saying through their own use of the miracle stories. Now, as we have seen, this does not mean that it must necessarily be the same as their message, for that would deny that element of dialogue which we have found to be at the heart of our use of the gospels. Nevertheless, it has to be a message which is worked out in dialogue with what the evangelists were really saying. Otherwise, we shall end up with something which is wholly other than their proclamation and which therefore at this point at any rate is not making proper use of the New Testament.

Secondly, our preaching must help our congregations to come to a legitimate approach to the question of the history underlying the miracle stories, for, though we may say 'the message is the thing', and though we may rightly feel that in saying this we are being true to the evangelists' own insights, nevertheless, our place in the twentieth century will not prevent us from bringing the question 'What really happened?' to the fore. Our task therefore is to help our congregations to come to an approach which will enable them to enter honestly into the narratives, and to present some understanding of this to others as and when they are called upon to do so. Certainly there should be an open attempt by us to deal with the problems that these narratives raise.

And it is undoubtedly true that it is this latter point which will be uppermost in the minds of many of our hearers for it has very practical results upon our believing, our expectations, and our prayers. How we understand the miracles of Jesus will fashion our expectations now, and will inevitably affect the way we shape our intercessions. More than that, though, it will influence the way we came to terms with – not to solve but to find an approach to, a way of living with – the problem of suffering and pain. Our understanding of the biblical narratives will affect our approach to life as it now is, though also, and inevitably, our understanding of reality as we now experience it cannot in turn fail to bring some influence to bear upon our understanding of the biblical narratives themselves.

If we are to understand the evangelists on these two points – if we are to come to terms with their message and if we are to come to a right understanding of what most likely brought the stories into being – then it is essential that we should remember that those who told them were first-century men who were expressing their beliefs through the thought-forms of the first century and approaching their subject in the light of the outlook of their day. And as first-century men their outlook upon miracles was necessarily very different from ours. Four things in particular affected their beliefs at this point.

In the first place, their understanding of the world, their approach to physical things, was very different from ours. They lived and believed in what was virtually a plastic world, one which was completely open to the power of God and to that of the supernatural world in general. Their world was at the mercy of powers outside itself, open to be invaded, taken over, moulded and refashioned by both good spirits and bad. And such was the nature of the world in which they lived that they tended to see, in the first place at any rate, pre-eminent among them the work of evil spirits, of demons who took over both man and nature. The natural world lay open before the supernatural, and the powers of the divine were limited, not by some natural resistance inherent in the make-up of the physical, but only by the will power of the divine and by the existence of other, and alien, powers who also claimed the world of nature and of man as their own sphere of influence. Spirits and demons entered, not only into men and animals, but also into inanimate objects which they stirred up and to which they gave a life and a power which was not really distinguishable from that of known beings.

Secondly, the evangelists lived in a world where Hellenistic wonder workers and magic-men were all around them and where tales of the miraculous were frequent.[12] There is nothing to suggest that our evangelists would have denied the truth of these stories or that they would have doubted the reality of the miraculous events that were reported to have taken place in the Hellenistic world. Any doubts they and their readers would have had would have centred, not upon the fact of the miracles, but upon the character of the person who performed them. The miraculous itself would not have been the occasion of dispute. An interesting illustration of this outlook is provided by the story of the sons of Sceva in Acts 19. Jewish exorcists were using the name of Jesus to drive out evil spirits, but when these seven sons did this, the evil spirit was believed to have overpowered them and to have put them to flight. The reality of their actions – the reality of their miracles achieved through magic – was not denied, nor was it said to be of a completely different order from that experienced by the followers of Jesus.

In the third place, stories of miracles are also to be found in Jewish sources contemporary with our gospel records. Holy men were accepted and what were regarded as their supernatural powers were attributed to their oneness with God. Jewish sources lamented the relative scarcity of miracles in the present but they were nevertheless still experienced and anticipated in the light of the past and of the future when the Lord would again be openly at work.

Alongside these stories of contemporaries, there were also the accounts of the Old Testament miracles. In actual fact, the Old Testament is remarkably restrained in this direction, but, apart from the great miraculous events of which the Exodus was the supreme paradigm, there were stories of wonders surrounding the lives of Moses, the initiator and source of the law, of Elijah, the fountain-head of prophecy, and of Elisha the companion and successor of Elijah. These great figures of the Old Testament were understood by Christians to have found their fulfilment in Jesus, and therefore it was to be expected that he would accomplish works like, but greater than, theirs. Moses had fed the people, supplied water in drought, and had controlled the forces opposed to evil. Elijah and Elisha had healed the sick, fed the poor, and raised the dead.

All this therefore – their understanding of reality, and their acceptance of miracles in Hellenistic, Jewish, and biblical narratives and expectations – meant that they were in fact miracle-oriented, miracle-expectant, even, we might dare to say, 'miracle-happy'. They would have expected Jesus to have performed miracles. They would have anticipated them, would not have questioned their possibility, and would have 'seen' them easily for they would have been looking for their happening. In this they were completely different in outlook from us, for we would be inclined always to play down the miraculous; most of us have our own built-in 'devil's advocate' to put all the objections and to subject the report of the miraculous to the closest scrutiny. Anything less we would feel to be both naive and unworthy of true proclamation. So, for instance, we would almost inevitably make the drowning of the Gadarene swine an unfortunate accident and we would take a lot of convincing that it was otherwise. The first century on the other hand would have had no doubts here at all; the supernatural explanation was the obvious one; miracle was in a sense the most natural thing in the world;

But if this meant that they believed more about the miraculous than we do, it meant also that they believed less. Miracles were always expected and they would have seen them where we would have found none. But, because of this, though the miracles were always marvellous, a source of wonder and amazement, they were not for them that total break with the world of nature which we make them. They were less apart from what was happening generally, less decisive as an intervention from without, less 'other' than what we mean by miracle today. Their miracles were less unambiguous, less dramatic, less unusual, and therefore of themselves less extraordinary. The ancient world's interest would be centred less on the miracle itself than on the worker of it, and any incredulity that might arise would be directed, not at the event itself, but at the nature, origin, and status of the one who caused it. The world to them was one continuous miracle, and therefore in a sense what we mean by miracle was to them unknown, for the raising of the dead was not really of a different order from a healing, which of itself was not of a different order from an exorcism, which again was not of a different kind from the quieting of a disturbed soul. Some were greater than others, but all were of the same kind for all represented a divine power flowing into the plastic world of the physical. Healing, wholeness, resurrection were all accomplished as the divine spirit empowered the physical and moved it. Ancient man did not attempt to decide what divine power could or could not do, for, in theory at any rate, it could do anything. The physical had no built-in resistance to it – that was provided only by other anti-divine yet equally powerful inhabitants of the spirit world. The physical was a plaything in the hands of the warring spirits.[13]

So then as far as the early church and the evangelists were concerned, not only were miracles to be expected and seen in the life of Jesus, but for them such miracles did not cut Jesus off from his contemporaries in the way that we tend to believe that they did. Other peoples' miracles were accepted. Jesus' miracles therefore could not of themselves prove the evangelists' claims on his behalf. They could indeed offer corroborative evidence for their belief in him. Looked at from the perspective of faith, they could deepen and illuminate God's action in him, but of themselves, they could not give evidence on his behalf which could not be gainsaid. For Jesus' opponents could point to his miracles as proof of his demon possession. Jesus in reply is reported to have stated; 'If I by the finger of God cast out devils, then is the kingdom of God come upon you.' He appealed to them to look at himself and to see who was behind him. If they could answer 'God' then, and only then, could his miracles be accepted as marks of the presence of the kingdom of God in him. Of themselves, they did not authenticate him. Rather, he authenticated them. He himself alone – his life, character, authority, integrity – determined whether God was one with him or not.

His answer to the doubts of John the Baptist as it is found in Matthew 11 and in Luke 7 does not contradict this for, again, the miracles can supply only corroborative evidence. 'Blessed is he who is not, offended in me.' Only if the person of Jesus is embraced can his miracles – seen as a part of his whole life – be themselves accepted as marks of God's kingdom.

The witness of the gospels is clear. Jesus worked 'miracles'. But these of themselves did not set him apart from other men. Jesus was one in his actions with the nature of reality as it was understood in his day. Of themselves, the miracles did not prove anything. They were witnesses to him, but only faith could see their true significance. Even the Fourth Gospel, though it puts more weight upon them as a reason for believing, has to go on to accept that they are nevertheless ambiguous in their witness and that faith is needed to make them into real signs of the presence of God in him.

How should all this affect our preaching of the miracles? In the first place, it means that we proclaim them from the standpoint of those who already have faith in Jesus. We have already been grasped by him and we look upon the miracle stories, not as events which themselves justify a faith or bring it into being, and certainly not as evidence which can prove Jesus or even commend him to others, but rather as witnesses of the early church to the nature of Jesus as they understood him, and as proclamations of what they knew from experience had been granted to them as they entered into that salvation brought by him. They looked at the miracles and used them as pointers to something greater, the real evidence for which was based, not on the miracles, but on the whole of that experience. We can use them as corroborative evidence for our belief in Jesus as we see what the early church was proclaiming through them and as their proclamation makes a point of contact with what we know of him now.

For the evangelists found their interest in the miracle stories controlled – not by the details of wonders that had happened in the past – but by their present beliefs about Jesus and by their experience of him now. They recounted them in the service of their present proclamation and in the light of what they knew had happened in their midst. Their primary concern and interest was in the miracle stories, not as events in the life of Jesus (for that would not in itself have made Jesus any different from many other men), but in them as a present witness to the living Lord.

The truth of this is seen clearly when their stories are studied carefully. We have already seen how John's story of the raising of Lazarus subordinates the past event to the present proclamation and that what on first reading appear to be details pointing to the events of history are there in fact to move the proclamation forward. At Cana, Jesus' dialogue with his mother and the evangelists own concluding comments again compel the narrative to be interpreted primarily as an unfolding of the evangelist's understanding of Jesus' saving work. The same is true of the synoptic stories.

The miracle stories should always be approached in the first place with the aim of uncovering the message of the evangelists. Then they can be used by us as vehicles of our own proclamation. Like the evangelists, we use them within the community of faith to deepen our own and our contemporaries' faith in Jesus. They can be preached as illustrations – almost, indeed, as parables – of the meaning of Jesus for us now. They can be used, not to prove Jesus (for they have never done that), not even as reasons for believing in him, but to unpack the manner and significance of his Lordship over us, and to illustrate the way of discipleship as it is based upon faith in him. In approaching the stories in this way, we will be true to the evangelists and we will work out our own understanding of the significance of the individual stories in dialogue with them.

There is, however, a necessary warning to be given at this stage. Our preaching must be based upon what the evangelists really were proclaiming through these stories for, if it isn't, there is a real danger of our trivializing the message that can come from them. It does, in fact, become all too easy to trivialize both their message and our own.[14] Such a trivialization has over the years often occurred in the interpretation of the parables whenever these were divorced from their link with Jesus' proclamation of the kingdom of God, and so were allowed to degenerate into somewhat innocuous stories about general moral truths. The same is true of our handling of the miracle stories, for they can all too easily be loosed from the evangelists' real proclamation of God's action in Jesus to become instances of his love and demands for compassion on our part.

We must not trivialize the miracles either by making them into something that we can easily grasp as an event, or by reducing their message into one of appreciation of Christ's concern which is then put forward for our imitation. For the evangelists, the miracles are real points of disclosure of the otherness of Jesus, of his mission, and of his saving act. They are recounted through faith and are set out as moments when the divine action in him can by faith be discovered, seen, and responded to. They are moments of the numinous, of awe, not – we must remember – because they state things which no one else could do, but because they are moments when this world becomes open to the divine world, when this world points to the actions of the other world, when the other world becomes visible in the here and now. They are what Bishop Ian Ramsey called disclosure situations, points of discernment, when the ice can break or the penny can drop. They sum up and express – for those who have eyes to see – the nature and manner of God's saving action in the Christ and of his demand upon those who would follow him.

But did the miracles really happen? The first century may have put no emphasis upon this point for such a question would not have occurred to them. For them, of course they happened; they were happening all the time. We, however, are twentieth-century men and women and this is a question which will trouble many of our listeners and is therefore one which must be tackled somewhere along the line by us.

The evangelists would certainly have maintained that they happened – that they were real events in history. They would not have questioned the traditions they received and, even if they actually made up any of the narratives themselves, their basis for this would have been an understanding of what 'must' have happened and therefore of what did in fact really occur.

We, however, cannot share their confidence here. In the first place, our understanding of reality and of the place of the physical within it is very different from theirs and we can therefore no longer anticipate miracles in the way that they did and so see them frequently around us. We are bound to be more hesitant, more critical. Secondly, we cannot expect things to have happened to Jesus, or expect things to have been done by him, simply because these were prophesied or foreshadowed in the Old Testament. We look at the Old Testament differently and no longer feel that it is legitimate to use it in this way. Thirdly, the way they handled the miracle stories, the way they subordinated them to their proclamation and wrote them up in the service of that, means that our chance of getting back to what really happened is slim. Their freedom in handling the miracle stories means that we cannot easily get back to what happened; our own hesitancy about miracles makes us doubly cautious here, and their ability to see miracles all around them makes us wonder about the literal acceptance of what they put before us.

Our doubts therefore are of such a kind that we cannot be certain that any one miracle happened in the way that the evangelists say it did, or even in fact, that that actual miracle happened at all. We must rather be agnostic about what actually happened at any one point in the story of Jesus. Every miracle story has to be treated individually as far as the question of determining what happened is concerned, though, by contrast, when the question of significance is being discussed, the individual story must be treated in the light of the whole series of miracle stories and in the light of the evangelists' total proclamation. But we have to be agnostic and to say that we do not know what actually happened as the basis of the individual stories. Because, in themselves, the miracles were not such remarkable events for the evangelists, they did not subject them to the scrutiny or careful factual description that we would have liked.

What we will not do however is to go in for that kind of rather pointless speculation which tries to discover some kind of relatively natural event which could have formed the basis of the tale of wonder. So we will not call the feeding of the five thousand a miracle of sharing and use it to point out the remarkable impact that Jesus had upon his fellow men. We will not use John's story of Jesus' walking upon the water to justify our belief that the Lord was really walking alongside the water, and we will not talk about remarkable occurrences of electric storms to explain the evangelists' accounts of Jesus' stilling of the storm. Again, we will not try to explain that Jairus' daughter was not really dead – that Jesus had more insight than his fellow-men. We just do not have the basis, the facts, for engaging in such speculation, and as preaching it can offer little or nothing to our congregations. Better it is to take the narrative as it stands and to see it as arising out of the creative response of the early church to their overwhelming apprehension that Jesus was their Lord and to their certainty that he brought them that wholeness and life which could come only from God. It is better that we should preach *that* as the ultimate basis for the coming into being of these stories rather than that we should try to see their origins in a series of fanciful, possible happenings which in the end can point only to a set of fortuitous events interpreted by a number of naive wishful-thinkers. We must pay the evangelists the compliment of taking their proclamation seriously, of trying to get inside their enthusiasms, their convictions, and their faith. If we cannot in all honesty base our response on real miraculous events in the life of Jesus – and our texts quite simply do not give us the means of doing that – then we should base it upon the faith of the early church as they, from their outlook and from their understanding, proclaimed their conviction in the present Lordship of Jesus in this way and by these means. The ultimate 'miracle' for our consideration is the faith of the early church in Jesus. It is this which demands a judgment from us – whether we can see it as based on reality – whether it is a mark of the 'finger of God' – or whether it is impelled by something else. If we can say that it is of God, that for us it is true, then we can share in their understanding of the significance of the miracles even if we cannot share in their understanding of what must have happened. The question we ask of our congregations is whether they can so learn from the faith of the early church, as that is expressed through the evangelists, that they can be enriched by it and in turn link up with it to make their own response to Jesus as Lord.

But, if we have to be agnostic about the particular narratives, what about the wider question – did Jesus in fact work miracles? Here we come down to the question, not of interpretation, but of fact: Did Jesus really heal the sick, cast out what were believed to be demons, still the storm, feed the hungry, and did he really raise the dead? Did Jesus work what *we* would see as miracles, for that is in fact what the gospels claim he did?

The evidence for raisings of the dead is in fact very slim and such narratives as do occur seem, as in the case of the raising of Lazarus and of the widow's son at Nain, to be controlled by theological proclamation or, as with the raising of Jairus' daughter, to have become 'hardened' in the telling. Only a hesitant answer to our question therefore is possible but, when it is given, it has to be one which suggests that such narratives bear witness more to beliefs and convictions about the nature of the new life found in Jesus than to actual historical events in his ministry. The same historical agnosticism must surround our approach to the nature miracles. Again it seems likely that theological conviction, religious insight, and Old Testament prefigurations have been brought together in narratives that proclaim the significance of Jesus for the early church.

Exorcisms and healings however are of a different order. Behind them would seem to stand real recollections of Jesus' authority and power. They witness to the fact that in him men encountered God's presence, his wholeness, and his life. In him men were confronted with the reality of God to find newness and release, and that the resulting wholeness should at least in some cases have permeated out to embrace the physical can only with difficulty be denied. With our modern understanding we would perhaps avoid the use of the word miracle: we would possibly see some explanation in the realm of the psychological and in the interaction of the body and mind of man. But the result would be no less significant for us than it would have been for the gospel narrators. In Jesus, men were confronted with the full reality of God's presence and in him therefore they were grasped by the wholeness of God's life and by the fullness of his recreating action.

We are in a better position to appreciate what the evangelists were proclaiming when they recorded their stories of miracles than were our predecessors.[15] Our awareness of the different outlook between them and us means that we are more able to understand what they were doing, that we have a better chance of seeing through their eyes so that we are in less danger of making them conform to standards fashioned by our own day and outlook, and that we can make a response which is both appropriate to them and also consistent with our place in the twentieth-century world.

EPILOGUE

Good News for Us

What are the implications of that understanding of the gospels that we have been trying to unfold in these chapters? How should it alter our overall outlook? How does this way of looking at the gospels affect our approach to the gospel itself? What is it saying to us which will enable us to enter more deeply into the work of God in Christ and so to be more effective channels of his saving grace? These are the questions which the parish priest will ask of the critic if he is to go on to try to take his findings seriously.[1]

They will certainly alter the 'feel' of our message, the overall context in which we disseminate it, and the tone and manner in which we proclaim it. They will not leave us with less confidence about the truth of what we proclaim but will make us base our convictions on a trust which accepts that we know only in part and that we walk by faith and not by sight. We will acknowledge that we see but the outskirts of God's ways and that we live in a hope of that which is not yet made fully visible. Our proclamation will be more sensitive to the difficulties it arouses, more questioning of its assumptions, and more aware of its significance as response to something which, by its very nature, cannot make such a response inescapable. It will be less strident, more humble than it was before; not less convinced but more understanding of the nature of the conviction, and more aware of the hiddenness of that on which it is based. If to the congregation it is expressed primarily in the form of a challenge to enter into the full implications of that by which they have been grasped, to those outside the believing community it will take the form of an invitation which, whilst recognizing the difficulties involved in acceptance, will nevertheless offer a stance which can lead to faith and commitment as it brings life and freedom in its train.

In some way this new understanding will make us less assertive than we were before. That certainly does not mean that we are less committed, for we remain men and women who have been grasped by God, those who share in a living faith which has inspired and impelled men of countless generations whose lives have been touched by God and enriched by his grace. But it does mean that we are more aware of the nature of our faith as response to things which have happened in our midst, things which by their nature cannot of themselves give proof of that to which we believe they testify and which cannot therefore of themselves demonstrate that value which we are led to place upon them. Reality and truth are given to them, not by sight but by faith, and our response finds its truth not in assurance but in pilgrimage. It is our surrender, our setting out on the way, which brings conviction, and it is our journey in faith which underlines for us its truth.

It will make us more understanding of those outside the community of faith, and more sensitive in our preaching to them for it will mean that we approach them as fellow-travellers on the way, as ones who are seeking ever more fully to understand the truth, as those who are striving to be ever more open to the implications of all that was begun in that obscure corner of the globe nearly two thousand years ago. That what happened then has often been misunderstood we may acknowledge – that in its name many evils have been perpetrated and many prejudices unleashed. Nevertheless, behind it all there has come into being a community of men and women who have found their life and their hope in Jesus and who have been unable to explain their experience in any other way than by a confession that they have been grasped by God in him. Our understanding and our experience join us to them so that we too can see in the events of his ministry, death, and resurrection, and in the life of the community these brought into being, nothing less than the action of God himself, of a God who draws near to men in a personal way and so unites them to his own being. We cannot explain either the life of Jesus or the response to him in any less a way than that they are in fact the actions of God himself, a God who without them would be so totally hidden as to be quite unworthy of belief. But Jesus and all that surrounds him gives us the confidence to go on, the reason for believing in a God behind the world, and the call to a commitment to him. The truth of this is discovered in the way of discipleship.

Such a discipleship does not take away our difficulties and it certainly does not make belief in God either easy or obvious. But it does make it real – it makes faith a viable possibility and establishes our discipleship as a living commitment which offers light in the darkness and life in the face of death. It is a faith which can live with the ambiguities of life as these are found in the lives of so many of our contemporaries and as we must be prepared to accept them into our own.

The modern critical understanding of the gospels enables us to walk around the wards of a modern hospital and to share in its life – in the realities of its suffering as well as the acts of heroism and compassion by those who would feel unable to call themselves Christians – and to believe that underneath it all there is a God of love. It enables us to stand in a crematorium chapel or at a grave-side and to have faith in resurrection as the fact of Jesus calls us to our own future in the God who stands behind both him and us. It enables us with Paul to proclaim our conviction that 'neither life nor death, nor angels, nor principalities nor powers, nor heights nor depths, can separate us from the love of God in Christ Jesus our Lord'. It enables us to express our faith that life is both meaningful and purposeful and that what appears to fall is taken up into the love, the reality, and the eternity of God's nature and God's life.

The work of the modern critics enables us to give full value to the evidence both of the scriptures and of our experience of living – an experience which must not centre upon our life alone but which must extend to include that of others also. The way of approaching the gospels that we have tried to unfold has this merit – that the experience of the individual is linked to the experience of the believing community which is itself worked out in relation to the experience of those amongst whom it lives.

For the preaching of the gospel must always be sensitive to the problems of those outside, not only as they look at and try to assess the reality of the message we proclaim but also as they attempt to link their experience of life, as it meets and embraces them, to the significance of the message as we deliver it. We must accept that the way of faith is not obvious, that it asks for a surrender which is not openly justified and clearly demanded. The commitment which we ask of those outside the church is much more demanding than we often appear to acknowledge for it entails a cross which not only means a total reversal of attitudes, a total upending of standards, a complete about-turn in expectations, but it does so in the name of a conviction which by its very nature cannot show that what it proclaims is demonstrable and obviously true. Nothing less than a recognition of this can amount to what embracing the cross really means.

Our message then will be appeal rather than propoganda; it will invite rather than demand, it will offer rather than cajole. Its manner will be reasonable rather than blustering, gentle rather than harsh, servicing rather than assertive. Its instrument will be the key rather than the bludgeon. It will offer rather than thrust. It will bring gifts and will not be easily offended when these are rejected or not even recognized. Above all, the message will be one of those who together seek after truth and look for a way of walking in the midst of perplexities. It offers a contribution – indeed *the* contribution – but does not assert that its contribution cannot be scrutinized, added to, even in part remade by those who bring to it their own insights and their own understanding.

It will of course challenge for it calls for repentance – that is a complete reversal of what is expected or looked for, a complete about turn in attitude to life. But the challenge is not to be separated from the gift, for that would cease to make the gospel good news; it would be following in the way of John the Baptist rather than in the way of Jesus. Jesus proclaimed repentance in the face of the coming of the kingdom but his actions in actually bringing the kingdom demonstrate that grace itself actually brings about the repentance which, without it, can mistake the nature of the God before whom it stands, and so make repentance itself into a work. The disclosure situation, the discernment, the insight must precede the repentance to make it real. Peter in Luke's story in chapter 5 of his gospel could find response only after he had been enabled to see the reality that Jesus represented. What caused Jesus to be so much at odds with those around him was precisely his insistence that the gift preceded the demand. Such a priority upended both natural justice and religious standards; it drove a coach and horses through established outlooks and left the way open for untidiness, blurred standards, and a free approach which could follow no clearly defined rules but which was based on the prodigal generosity of God. For grace is not cheap but free. A free gift however can never demand that it be rightly used before it be given. The father could not be sure that the younger son would not yet again spurn his sonship; Jesus could not be certain that the woman taken in adultery would not repeat the escapade; those who went to work in the vineyard at the eleventh hour may well have been the idlers of the village. Forgiveness puts the forgiver wholly at risk. He leaves himself completely open to being taken for yet another ride. Yet it is in that total acceptance, in that total removal of barriers, that the real point of discernment comes. The total gift can alone express the total nature of the demand that is implicit in it.

What the biblical critic is challenging us to rediscover is the true nature of a faith which has the cross at its centre; he is compelling us to

can be turned down

a greater understanding of the meaning of the cross and to a fuller realization of what is meant in the dominical command that we must take up the cross for ourselves. This is undoubtedly his most important contribution towards a recovery of faith.

In the first place, as we have seen, he enables us to see more clearly than we did before just what the cross meant for Jesus. Jesus did not have a clearly defined, fully worked out understanding of just what the cross meant for him. He went forward in faith, and his faith issued in obedience. He believed in vindication, but just how it was to be achieved he did not know. His surrender did not protect him from despair. The Epistle to the Hebrews brings this out clearly: 'In the days of his flesh, Jesus offered up prayers and supplications with loud cries and tears, to him who was able to save him from death, and he was heard for his godly fear. Although he was a Son, he learned obedience through what he suffered; and being made perfect, he became the source of eternal salvation to all who obey him, being designated by God a high priest after the order of Melchizedek.'

That is the way that we are called upon to follow. The resurrection is the vindication of Jesus, but it is not one which cancels out the cross for it makes the crucified Jesus, not a figure of the past, but of the present. The risen Jesus bears the marks of his cross, he is known as he unfolds the necessity of his sufferings and as he presides at the eucharistic meal which embraces his death as well as his resurrection. In Hebrews, he offers his sacrifice continually in heaven; in Revelation, he is the Lamb who has been slain. In the New Testament as a whole, the resurrection is seen as the making present of the cross rather than its cancellation.

The church therefore is the body of Christ only insofar as she bears the marks of his cross; she is filled with his resurrection power only as she is united to him crucified. She shows him to the world only as she goes forward with the cross, not as some vindicating power which takes the form of an earthly, visible activity – whether it be the conquering outlook of a Constantine, the triumphalism of nineteenth-century missionary hymns, or the assertiveness of some plan of church growth – but as a way of life, a pilgrimage of faith, a commitment to surrender, a way of disinterested service, of purity of heart. The church's relationship to the cross should be one, not of having, but of being.

But it is just this understanding of the cross that we try to avoid. We want our Jesus to be more obvious to us than he was to his contemporaries. We want God's action to be more demonstrable now than it was to the early church. We want a more solid basis for our faith, more grounds for our response than those which were available to them. We want records of God's action to give us evidence which is of the nature of hard, objective facts. We want a proclamation of the significance of Jesus which can be accepted as final, authoritative, and complete. In short, what we want is a God who acts in some way other than through a cross.

The early church, however, had none of these benefits. Jesus was not demonstrably provable either to them or to their contemporaries. Nothing could guarantee him; only faith could acknowledge him, and that entailed a surrender, a willingness to follow in his path. But for them, at least at first, there was the hope that some full visible demonstration of his power would come soon. They looked to an early parousia to provide this but, when it failed to materialize, they had to think again and to find their justification for believing in the only visible evidence they had – the living faith of the community as it found life through him and as it was enabled to accept his hidden life as the life of the Lord. The gospels were written to help them to continue in their initial conviction and to grow in their understanding of the nature of his lordship. Mark found confidence in a hope for the future; Matthew found his conviction expressed in the life of the believing community; Luke saw the presence of the Spirit of the risen Lord in the history of the outreach; John found eternal life in response to Jesus' revelation of God.

But the life of the community, the experience of the church, was the ultimate test of the truth of the response. Their proclamation was itself an act of faith in that hidden life of Jesus which was climaxed in and characterized by the cross. By showing to us the nature of the gospels as testimony and by calling us to share in their response, modern criticism of the gospels has exposed the true nature of faith, and so enabled the true nature of Christ's call to take up our cross to be clearly heard. By revealing the real nature of Christ's hiddenness, it enables a true understanding of Christian commitment. It puts before us the cross in all its starkness, its powerlessness and defencelessness, and will not let us avoid the total surrender which this demands of us. In this way, it makes us open to the true resurrection life of Christ which alone will bring life to both us and the world.

That then is the gospel critics' call to the church – to find our life as we are prepared to let it go, to find faith as we are ready to launch out into the deep, to discover the power of the cross as we are willing to find our hope in nothing else. They are challenging us to deepen our understanding and to re-examine our way of life.

And this is the way that was put before us by the apostle to the Gentiles himself. For him, the marks of a true apostle were seen, not in strength but in weakness. 'I will all the more gladly boast of my weaknesses, that the power of Christ may rest upon me. For the sake of Christ then I am content with weaknesses, insults, hardships, persecutions, and calamities; for when I am weak, then I am strong.' The church is called to live 'as unknown and yet well known, as dying, and behold we live; as punished and yet not killed; as sorrowful, yet always rejoicing; as poor, yet making many rich; as having nothing, and yet possessing everything'. Modern criticism of the gospels helps to reveal the true nature of our riches and so makes clear that style of life to which we are called. It will not allow us to parade a false triumphalism and it will not allow us to sidestep that true weakness which alone reflects the real nature of the cross. For, to quote Paul yet again, 'We preach Christ crucified, a stumbling-block to Jews and folly to Gentiles, but to those who are called, both Jews and Greeks, Christ the power of God and the wisdom of God. For the foolishness of God is wiser than men, and the weakness of God is stronger than men.' Whenever we seek to make the gospel more obvious than it really is, whenever we seek to move beyond the cross (which is really to move away from it), whenever we seek to avoid its essential ambiguity, its inescapable stumbling-block, whenever we seek to fashion ourselves by standards which are other than its own, we proclaim less than God's saving activity and we are turning the truth of God into a lie.

But what of our congregations? Are we imposing too great a strain upon them? Are we putting upon them more than they can bear? For, after all, many in our congregations (perhaps even most of them) are there because of some need which is met by what we offer them in the name of Christ. In the community of faith they often find a home which is denied them elsewhere. Here they can become persons with a life, and perhaps even an importance, of their own. Here they can find some fulfilment which elsewhere escapes them. Can this newer understanding help them and so enable us to meet our pastoral obligations to them? It can, for it faces the ambiguities of life and meets these with a confidence which comes from its true understanding of the love of God as it sees this revealed through Jesus. It expresses the hurt only to accept it, and through acceptance, to make it bearable. It unites them to the truth of life itself, and takes up its darkness into the light of God.

And it helps the congregation as a whole to grow into that maturity to which we are summoned and which is in fact so often there, waiting to

be set free. For undoubtedly we parish priests are often guilty of pater-
nalism in general and of that form of it in particular which transfers our
own fears to our congregations and imposes our own hesitations and
insecurities upon them. We are often hindrances to, rather than aids
towards, maturity. But our congregations are so often much tougher,
much more realistic, much more discriminating, much less brittle than
we allow. Of course there are the self-assured, the precocious and the
superior. But religiosity must have its bubble pricked in the interests of
the gospel. And the pastor will not be unmindful of those who will be
genuinely hurt by his new openness; he will be sensitive to those whose
faith is based upon a genuine belief in the facts of the gospels seen as
historical witnesses to actual events. Such folk will need his patience and
his love and he will make sure that he himself is really embracing the
cross at this point.

But the hurt which we see in this kind of preaching will in fact be far
less than we imagine, for it is undoubtedly true that many in our congregations are far less uncritical than we sometimes believe. This way of
looking at the gospels is often seen as a release as well as a challenge, for
it enables difficulties to be faced openly, perplexities to be aired and sur-
mounted, and the questionings of others to be entered into. Above all,
it uncovers the true nature of Christian belief and exposes its basis in
the faith and life of the believing community. The experience and commitment of both the individual and the group are allowed to speak for
themselves and the resurrection life of the Lord is enabled to run free
into the realities of the present.

FOR FURTHER READING

Two useful books which offer an instructive way into the New Testament in general and into the gospels in particular:

T. G. A. Baker, *What is the New Testament?*, SCM Press 1969

Brian E. Beck, *Reading the New Testament Today*, Lutterworth 1977

Commentaries which might be suggested as offering valuable insights into the practical use of the gospels:

H. Benedict Green, *The Gospel According to Matthew*, New Clarendon Bible, Oxford University Press 1975

D. E. Nineham, *St Mark*, Pelican Books 1963

E. Earle Ellis, *The Gospel of Luke*, New Century Bible, Marshall, Morgan and Scott 1966

Barnabas Lindars, *The Gospel of John*, New Century Bible, Marshall, Morgan and Scott 1972

Important books on Jesus:

C. K. Barrett, *Jesus and the Gospel Tradition*, SPCK 1967

John Knox, *The Death of Christ*, Collins 1958, Fontana 1967

James P. Mackey, *Jesus: the Man and the Myth*, SCM Press 1979

Eta Linnemann, *Parables of Jesus*, SPCK 1966

Joachim Jeremias, *Rediscovering the Parables*, SCM Press 1966

Helpful books on the problem of New Testament interpretation:

D. E. Nineham, *The Use and Abuse of the Bible*, Macmillan 1976

Morna Hooker and Colin Hickling (eds), *What about the New Testament?*, SCM Press 1975

Patrick Henry, *New Directions in New Testament Study*, SCM Press 1980

NOTES

Prologue : The Preacher and the Critic

1. See the preface of R. P. C. Hanson, *Mystery and Imagination*, SPCK 1976.
2. A survey of modern biblical interpretation with a useful critique of Biblical Theology is to be found in James Barr, *The Bible in the Modern World*, SCM Press 1973.
3. James D. Smart, *The Strange Silence of the Bible in the Church*, SCM Press 1970 gives a compelling account of this.
4. See the essay by Ivor Smith-Cameron, 'Faith and Mission', in Kathleen Jones (ed.), *Living the Faith*, Oxford University Press 1980.

1 Behind the Gospels

1 An important work which develops this theme is John Knox, *The Church and the Reality of Christ*, Collins 1962.
2. A useful account of form criticism is given by Ralph P. Martin, *New Testament Foundations* Volume 1, Paternoster 1975, pp. 119–38. This volume gives a most clear account of recent approaches to the gospels.
3. This is seen at its best in Adolf Harnack, *What is Christianity?*, 5th ed. Benn 1958.
4. See Morna Hooker, 'In his own Image?' in *What about the New Testament?* (ed.) Morna Hooker and Colin Hickling, SCM Press 1975.
5. R. H. Lightfoot was accustomed to describe the gospels as one of the fruits of the early church's failure of nerve.
6. See Howard C. Kee, *Christian Origins in Sociological Perspective*, SCM Press 1980.

2 The Synoptic Gospels

1. Patrick Henry, *New Directions in New Testament Study*, SCM Press 1979, pp. 53–5; John Bowden, *Voices in the Wilderness*, SCM Press 1977, pp. 42–57.
2. Norman Perrin, *What is Redaction Criticism?*, SPCK 1970. This is an interesting account of the subject though, unfortunately, it does not pay enough attention to the historical basis of the interpretation.

3. See, below, the discussion of the various evangelists' accounts of the rejection at Nazareth.

4. Reasons for accepting the priority of Mark are summarized in Martin, op. cit., pp. 140–3.

5. This position is argued by Xavier Léon-Dufour, *The Gospels and the Jesus of History*, Fontana edition 1970, and by John A. T. Robinson, *Redating the New Testament*, SCM Press 1976.

6. See the arguments for Proto-Luke in G. B. Caird, *Saint Luke*, Pelican Gospel Commentaries 1963, pp. 23–7.

7. H. Benedict Green, *The Gospel according to Matthew*, Oxford University Press 1975, p. 97.

8. See Ch. 6 of Eric Franklin, *Christ the Lord*, SPCK 1975.

9. Modern scholarship has emphasized the belief that the gospels, rather than being missionary tracts, were, in the first instance at any rate, written from within the church to the church.

10. A. E. Harvey calls his popular introduction to the New Testament '*Something Overheard*', Bible Reading Fellowship 1977.

11. A useful synopsis of the first three gospels is *Gospel Parallels*, (ed.) B. H. Throckmorton, Nelson 1957.

12. Various series of commentaries have been published recently. It is probably wise to be selective in making your choice, and a number of suggestions can be found in *For Further Reading* above p. 173.

13. See the introduction in E. Earle Ellis, *The Gospel of Luke*, New Century Bible 1966.

14. See the criticisms of Hooker, op. cit. pp. 28–44.

15. A most important book on this theme and one which repays very careful study is James D. G. Dunn, *Unity and Diversity in the New Testament*, SCM Press 1977.

16. See G. Bornkamm, *Jesus of Nazareth*, Hodder and Stoughton 1960, p. 167.

17. See the essay by John Fenton, 'The Preacher and the Biblical Critic' in *What about the New Testament?*

3 The Fourth Gospel

1. See William Temple's introduction in his *Readings in St John's Gospel*, Macmillan 1950.

2. This is well summarized in A. M. Hunter, *According to John*, SCM Press 1968.

3. Temple, op. cit., p. xviii.

4. This is the position expounded by R. H. Lightfoot, *St John's Gospel*, Oxford University Press 1956. The whole commentary is a mine of lucid insights which can well be carried over into devotional and expository occasions.

5. This insight is worked out by Barnabas Lindars, *The Gospel of John*, New Century Bible, Marshall, Morgan and Scott 1972.

6. This understanding forms the basis of an illuminating book by A. E. Harvey, *Jesus on Trial*, SPCK 1976.

7. See the treatment by James D. G. Dunn, *Unity and Diversity in the New Testament*, pp. 302–5.

4 A Question of History

1. The danger of this is seen in Perrin, *What is Redaction Criticism?*

2. An important work which deals with this question is I. Howard Marshall, *I Believe in the Historical Jesus*, Hodder and Stoughton 1977.

3. Reviews by parish priests of the critics' works often make this point.

4. See C. F. Evans, *Resurrection and the New Testament*, SCM Press 1970.

5. See the attempt at harmonization by C. F. D. Moule (ed.), *The Significance of the Message of the Resurrection for Faith in Jesus Christ*, SCM Press 1968. His whole article deserves careful consideration and is a most useful introduction to the whole question of the resurrection narratives.

6. See Marshall, op. cit., pp. 23–4.

7. C. K. Barrett, *Jesus and the Gospel Tradition*, p. 5.

8. See the treatment of Old Testament historical traditions in Gerhard von Rad, *Old Testament Theology*, Oliver and Boyd 1962.

9. Full value should be given to R. H. Lightfoot's comment in *History and Interpretation in the Gospels*, Hodder and Stoughton 1935, pp. 82–3.

10. This point is made by Patrick Henry, *New Directions*, Ch. 6.

11. A work that deserves serious attention is C. Leslie Mitton, *Jesus: the Fact Behind the Faith*, Mowbray 1975.

12. See J. C. Fenton's essay in *What about the New Testament?*

13. This is worked out in relation to the virginal conception of Jesus by Raymond E. Brown, *The Birth of the Messiah*, Geoffrey Chapman 1977.

14. See John Knox, *The Church and the Reality of Christ*.

15. This is drawn out most illuminatingly by James D. G. Dunn, *Unity and Diversity in the New Testament*.

5 A Word for Us

1. Eric Franklin, *Christ the Lord*.

2. A useful account is given by Anthony C. Thiselton, 'The New Hermeneutic' in *New Testament Interpretation*, (ed.) I. Howard Marshall, Paternoster Press 1977.

3. Norman Perrin, *Jesus and the Language of the Kingdom*, SCM Press 1976, pp. 120–7.

4. See Barr's criticisms in *The Bible in the Modern World*, p. 74.

5. A useful and balanced discussion of the problem is that by Michael Ramsey, *Jesus and the Living Past*, Oxford University Press 1980.

6. No one has done more to make us aware of the very real nature of the problem than has Dennis Nineham and, in spite of the opprobrium that has been heaped upon him as a result, we should be grateful for his warning on the dangers of feeling that we can easily come to grips with ancient writings and understand them in the way that their contemporaries did or, indeed, in a way that is legitimate for us. As well as his *The Use and Abuse of the Bible* see his volume of essays, *Explorations in Theology* 1, SCM Press 1977.

7. Leonard Hodgson, *For Faith and Freedom*, Vol 2, Blackwell 1957, p. 12.

8. Rudolf Bultmann, see H. W. Bartsch (ed.), *Kerygma and Myth*, SPCK 1953, p. 5.

9. This is worked out by G. W. H. Lampe, *God as Spirit*, Oxford University Press 1977, pp. 153–7.

6 Preaching Jesus

1. See J. Austin Baker's important description of the two different understandings of the nature of the Christian response in *The Foolishness of God*, Fontana edition p. 164.

2. See how this is worked out by Don Cupitt, *Jesus and the Gospel of God*, Lutterworth 1979.

3. This is worked out more fully by Don Cupitt, *The Debate About Christ*, SCM Press 1979.

4. See Henry J. Cadbury's working out of this in *The Peril of Modernizing Jesus*, SPCK 1962.

5. Otto Betz, *What Do We Know about Jesus?*, SCM Press 1968, p. 89.

6. Different approaches to the Son of Man question can be seen in R. H. Fuller, *The Foundations of New Testament Christology*, Lutterworth 1965, and Geza Vermes, *Jesus the Jew*, Collins 1973.

7. A useful discussion can be found in John Ziesler, *The Jesus Question*, Lutterworth 1980.

8. E. Käsemann, *Essays on New Testament Themes*, SCM Press 1964, pp. 37 and 40.

9. C. H. Dodd, *The Parables of the Kingdom*, Nisbet 1935.

10. See E. Linnemann, *Parables of Jesus*, SPCK 1966. Her work deserves most careful reading.

11. J. Jeremias, *New Testament Theology*, SCM Press 1971, pp. 36–7: 61–8.

12. A useful account of Jesus' teaching on the Kingdom is given in G. E. Ladd, *Jesus and the Kingdom*, SPCK 1966. His thinking about Jesus and the future, however, should be supplemented by W. G. Kümmel, *Promise and Fulfilment*, SCM Press 1957.

13. See Perrin, *Jesus and the Language of the Kingdom*.

14. Nineham's comments in *The Use and Abuse of the Bible*, Ch. 7.

15. See A. L. Moore, *The Parousia in the New Testament*, E. J. Brill, Leiden 1966.

16 C. H. Dodd, *The Founder of Christianity*, esp. pp. 105ff.
17. C. K. Barrett, *Jesus and the Gospel Tradition*, pp. 39–41.
18. See the careful summary by C. F. D. Moule, *The Origin of Christology*, Cambridge University Press 1977, p. 109.

7 'We Have Seen His Glory'

1. See the careful and sensitive statement by Vincent Taylor in *The Life and Ministry of Jesus*, Macmillan 1954, p. 19.
2. This is the position of J. McHugh, *The Mother of Jesus in the New Testament*, Darton, Longman & Todd 1975, and, more popularly expressed in David Winter, *But This I Can Believe*, Hodder and Stoughton 1980.
3. Raymond E. Brown, *The Birth of the Messiah*, is supremely important on the infancy narratives.
4. See Eric Franklin, *Christ the Lord*, pp. 80–7.
5. A very useful work on this is Peter De Rosa, *Jesus Who Became Christ*, Collins 1975.
6. De Rosa, op. cit., pp. 54–7.
7. This is best worked out in a careful and understandable way by Geoffrey Lampe in G. Lampe and D. MacKinnon, *The Resurrection*, Mowbray 1966.
8. See Lampe's statement in the above work.
9. See Neville Clark, *Interpreting the Resurrection*, SCM Press 1967, esp. pp. 97ff.
10. A good account is found in Moule's introduction to the volume *The Significance of the Message of the Resurrection for Faith in Jesus Christ*.
11. Lampe in *God as Spirit* moves towards this third view.
12. See Jeremias, *New Testament Theology*, pp. 86ff.
13. See Nineham, *The Use and Abuse of the Bible*, pp. 32–5.
14. Bruce Kay, *The Supernatural in the New Testament*, Lutterworth 1977 comes near to doing this.
15. See Eduard Schweizer, *Jesus*, SCM Press 1971, esp. pp. 43ff.

Epilogue : Good News for Us

1. See the carefully worked out statement of this in John Fenton and Michael Hare Duke, *Good News*, SCM Press 1976.

INDEX